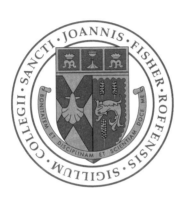

Lavery Library

St. John Fisher College

Rochester, New York

Black, White,
and *Huckleberry Finn*

Black, White,
and *Huckleberry Finn*

Re-imagining the American Dream

Elaine Mensh and Harry Mensh

THE UNIVERSITY OF ALABAMA PRESS

Tuscaloosa and London

Copyright © 2000
The University of Alabama Press
Tuscaloosa, Alabama 35487-0380
All rights reserved
Manufactured in the United States of America

1 2 3 4 5 6 7 8 9 . 08 07 06 05 04 03 02 01 00

Cover design by Erin Kirk New

∞

The paper on which this book is printed meets the minimum requirements of
American National Standard for Information Science–Permanence of Paper for
Printed Library Materials, ANSI Z39.48-1984.

Library of Congress Cataloging-in-Publication Data

Mensh, Elaine
Black, white, and Huckleberry Finn : reimagining the American
dream / Elaine mensh and Harry Mensh.
p. cm.
Includes bibliographical references (p. 149) and index.
ISBN 0-8173-0995-0 (alk. paper)
1. Twain, Mark, 1835–1910. Adventures of Huckleberry Finn.
2. Literature and society—United States—History—19th century.
3. Twain, Mark, 1835–1910—Political and social views. 4. Adventure
stories, American—History and criticism. 5. National characteristics,
American, in literature. 6. Fugitive slaves in literature. 7. Race
relations in literature. 8. Afro-Americans in literature. 9. Whites in
literature. I. Mensh, Harry II. Title.
PS1305 .M46 2000
813´.4—dc21
99-6204

British Library Cataloguing-in-Publication Data available

To Ashley Montagu
With unending appreciation

Though we do not wholly believe it yet, the interior life is a real life, and the intangible dreams of people have a tangible effect on the world.

—James Baldwin, *Nobody Knows My Name*

Contents

Acknowledgments

This time around, it means even more to us to thank Curtis L. Clark for his acuity, judgment, and, not least, concern. Our appreciation goes to Louis J. Budd and Tom Quirk, who read the manuscript for The University of Alabama Press, for their probing critiques and valuable suggestions. Thanks also to Elizabeth May, Suzette Griffith, and all of the Press staff members who worked with us for their professionalism, support, and friendliness. And, finally, thanks to Jonathan Lawrence for his perceptive copyediting.

Black, White,
and *Huckleberry Finn*

Introduction

Imagine that you enter a parlor. You come late. When you arrive,
others have long preceded you, and they are engaged in a heated
discussion, a discussion too heated for them to pause and tell you
exactly what it is about. . . . You listen for a while, until you decide
that you have caught the tenor of the argument; then you put in
your oar. Someone answers; you answer him; another comes to
your defense; another aligns himself against you, to either the embarrassment or gratification of your opponent, depending upon the
quality of your ally's assistance. However, the discussion is intermi-
nable. The hour grows late, you must depart. And you do depart,
with the discussion still vigorously in progress.[1]

This scene was conceived, in 1941, by a prominent literary critic
as an allegory for the discussion, pursued unendingly by Americans
from generation to generation, on culture. The scene appears to represent an exemplary discussion—intense, open. Upon reflection,
though, questions arise. Perhaps, rather than serving as a parable for
the American cultural discussion, the scene is a rendering of the discussion the critic took part in. Or, to be even more exact, a rendering
of that discussion from the critic's perspective.

For, considered from a different perspective, the dialogue's open-
ness turns out to be, if not illusory, at least severely circumscribed.
After all, you do not enter a parlor without an invitation. Moreover,

you are apt to be invited into the parlor only if you have achieved a certain status. While the connection between social class and participation in the discussion is clear, that between gender and participation is less so. Although a parlor is compatible with the presence of women, the critic's use of a male pronoun to denote the participants suggests a distinction between presence and participation. But whatever ambiguities attach to gender, none attaches to race: in that era, choosing a parlor as the metaphorical site of the cultural dialogue implied that the color line would be drawn at the door.

We do not mean to suggest, we must hastily add, that the critic chose the site with this consideration in mind; on the contrary, he was surely unaware of the way in which his metaphor mirrored the era's cultural conversation—or, rather, a dominant part of it. Beyond its boundaries lay another, a vital, part of the discussion. To bring this part into focus, let us do two things: keep the metaphorical premises, while changing "you" from a designation for those included to one for those excluded—African Americans of both genders:

If you are not guests in the parlor, it is not because you came late; on the contrary, you long preceded most of those already there. Had you entered, you would not have had to wait to learn what the discussion was about. You caught the tenor long ago. And, time and again, you put in your oar. Yet the sound it made, coming as it did from the outside, went for the most part unheard or unheeded by those inside. But however late the hour, you did not depart. As the forties moved into the fifties, you were still seldom a guest in the parlor. As the fifties moved on, though, what you said from the outside was being heard even in the parlor—including what you had to say about an American literary classic.

As time went on, you increasingly entered the debate over the classic from the inside as well as the outside. And as the debate continued, it became ever more evident that the argument over fictional black-white relations was also an argument over nonfictional black-white relations: over black images in white minds, unequal authority along racial lines, conflicting perceptions of black-white amity, and—because of the classic's unique place in the national consciousness—differing interpretations of the American dream.

I | The Trespassers

I

On September 4, 1957, National Guard troops ringed Little Rock's Central High School, which had been ordered to desegregate. They had been called up by the governor, who predicted, or promised, that "blood would run in the streets" if black children tried to enter. When eight of the children arrived, accompanied by two black and two white clergymen, they were confronted by the troops and a howling mob of men and women. The children were pushed and shoved, then informed by a National Guard captain that on orders of the governor they would not be allowed to enter. Escorted by the president of the State Conference of NAACP branches, a black woman, the children proceeded to the offices of the United States Attorney and the FBI.[1]

A ninth child had not been informed that the students were to come as a group. When she arrived alone, there were shouts from the mob, which now numbered about five hundred: "They're here! The niggers are coming!" "Get her! Lynch her!" The student tried several times to pass through the troops; on her last try, she was stopped with bayonets. The mob yelled, "No nigger bitch is going to get in our school." With the troops standing by impassively, someone screamed, "Get a rope and drag her over to this tree." A white-haired woman fought her way through the mob, shouting: "Leave this child alone! Why are you tormenting her? Six months from now you will hang your heads in shame." The mob hollered, "Another nigger-lover. Get out of here!"

The woman, a professor at a Little Rock college, stayed with the child until she could get her away on a bus. Joining with her to protect the child during the wait was the *New York Times* education editor, who was threatened as a "dirty New York Jew." In the next weeks, there were attacks on black men and women and on their homes, as well as assaults on black and white journalists. Finally, confronted with the Little Rock black community, which refused to surrender to the authorities or the mob, and also challenged by national and world opinion, the president acted to enforce the desegregation order; he federalized the Arkansas National Guard and directed the secretary of defense to send in regular troops as needed.[2]

The incident at Little Rock had myriad consequences, explicit and tacit. One of the latter appears to be an action taken by the New York Board of Education. Just eight days after the confrontation at Central High, the *New York Times* reported, in a front-page story, that the board had "quietly dropped" *Adventures of Huckleberry Finn* from approved textbook lists for elementary and junior high schools. The novel, the *Times* also related, could still be purchased for school libraries and used as a textbook in high schools. The story linked the board's action to objections from the NAACP. The NAACP denied having protested to the board, but acknowledged that it "strongly objected to the 'racial slurs' and 'belittling racial designations' in Mark Twain's works."[3]

Although there is no evidence that the NAACP protested directly to the board, objections from one or another source certainly reached the board. But the official in charge of curriculum development stated that no objections had come to her attention. She said the novel had been taken off the approved textbook list because, as the *Times* put it, it was "not really a textbook."[4] In giving this explanation, which was notable only for its surrealism (a book approved as a textbook was removed for not being a textbook), New York City school officials apparently believed they had converted a controversial move into an administrative correction, and so could escape responsibility for their own action.[5]

That there was little resemblance between an official story and the truth is hardly news, but the extreme ineptitude revealed in this story raises questions. Why was the board of education so utterly unprepared to offer even a remotely credible, let alone factual, explanation for its action on *Huck Finn?* One answer seems to be that school officials had been readied for the wrong battle, that is, for a skirmish essentially won by the time *Huck Finn* became required reading.

II

"Once we understand how they arose, we no longer see literary canons as *objets trouvés* washed up on the beach of history," observes Henry Louis Gates, Jr.[6] The point is aptly illustrated by *Huckleberry Finn*'s journey into the schools' literary canon. The journey, which spanned more than two decades, began with a study whose stated aim was to determine "the most effective ways of utilizing" the novel in junior high schools.[7] The study was followed, in 1931, by an edition published especially for junior high schools. In the introduction, the editors—speaking with the quaintness then deemed appropriate for addressing children—wrote: "In those early days Huck had but one friend who dared openly to seek his company, . . . Tom Sawyer. But today how different! . . . Then the parents tabooed Huck as a companion for their sons, but today the most respected of mothers open their doors to welcome in this wanderer."[8]

Since these lines descend from a supposedly more innocent time, it might seem they really were intended for children. But not only is it quite illogical to expect that children would be delighted by Huck's newfound respectability, it also seems odd to contrast the novel's respectability in the eyes of real parents with Huck's lack of it with fictional ones. Clearly, when the editors spoke of Huck's ostracism in his "early days," they had in mind not Huck's status in *Tom Sawyer,* but *Huck Finn*'s expulsion from the Concord Public Library in 1885 as the "veriest trash," "rough, coarse, and inelegant,"[9] unfit for "our pure-minded lads and lasses,"[10] and the copycat expulsions that followed.

The editors were Emily Fanning Barry, an English teacher at

Teachers College, and Herbert B. Bruner, who headed its Curriculum Construction Laboratory. Under the aegis of the publisher, Harper & Brothers, they conducted the study, which involved "thousands" of reports obtained from an unspecified number of teachers and pupils. The editors describe the student participants according to class, nationality, and location. Since they do not mention race, it is quite safe to assume "children" meant "white children."[11]

That this study undoubtedly included white children only does not mean the editors consciously sought to exclude black children. Their apparent absence from the study simply mirrored the exclusion of blacks from vast areas of American life. And even if the editors had been amazingly ahead of their time and wondered how black children might feel about *Huck Finn*, there would have been no reason to pursue the daring thought. Certainly it would have had no value for the publisher, given that black schools were likely to receive books handed down from white ones.

While the study, the classroom edition, and growing support from educators laid the groundwork for *Huck Finn* to become required reading, something more was needed to bring the effort to fruition. This arrived in the form of essays by Lionel Trilling (1948) and T. S. Eliot (1950) that provided the novel with the "academic respectability and clout" that assured its entry into the nation's classrooms, points out Peaches Henry.[12] Trilling, who launched what Jonathan Arac calls the "hypercanonization" of *Huck Finn*,[13] spoke of it as "one of the world's great books and one of the central documents of American culture."[14] Eliot termed it a "masterpiece."[15] Both, however, were concerned with defending it against the by now largely anachronistic morality charge. Eliot made the point fairly subtly by stating he had not read the book as a boy because his parents considered it unsuitable, while he also spoke of things in it that would delight boys. The matter is, though, handled quite explicitly by Trilling, who remarks that Huck is "really a very *respectable* person."[16]

Trilling also explicitly defended the novel against the "subversion of morality" charge. *Huck Finn*, he wrote, is "indeed a subversive book—no one who reads thoughtfully the dialectic of Huck's great moral crisis will ever again be wholly able to accept without some question" the "assumptions of the respectable morality by which he lives," nor see any distinction between the supposed "dictates of moral reason" and the "engrained customary beliefs of his time and place."[17] In Trilling's essay, engrained customary beliefs did not include whites' attitudes toward blacks; perfunctory in his approach to slavery, he was oblivious of its legacy.

As for the educators who advocated *Huck Finn* for the classroom, they surely believed they were taking a bold step to replace vapid children's books with a novel of many wonders. The wonders of the river. The wonder of a fictional boy whose voice "strikes the ear with the freshness of a real boy talking out loud."[18] A boy who is not merely a "bad boy" in the old, conventional sense, but one who can beat the grownups at their own dangerous games. So there seemed to be something in *Huck Finn* for every child. But there were also things the decision makers had not noticed. Nor did they seem to notice that, as time went on, racial matters had entered a state of acute flux, while their decision-making process had remained static, that is, monoracial.

The effort to establish *Huck Finn* as required reading, launched at a time of de jure segregation, culminated when this form of segregation had suffered a major blow. The novel's "entrenchment in the English curricula of junior and senior high schools coincided" with the decision in *Brown v. Board of Education*. Thus "desegregation and the civil rights movement deposited Huck in the midst of American literature classes which were no longer composed of white children only, but now were dotted with black youngsters as well," notes Henry. These youngsters, whose opinions of the novel had previously evoked zero interest, would soon become *Huck Finn*'s "most persistent and formidable foe."[19]

III

The day after it reported the New York Board of Education's action on *Huckleberry Finn*, the *Times* ran an editorial, "Huck Finn's Friend Jim." It described the novel as "one of the deadliest satires" ever written on "some of the nonsense that goes on with the inequality of races." Although the black character is introduced as "'Miss Watson's big nigger, named Jim,'" that "was the Missouri vernacular of that day." Moreover, Jim is a "warm human being, lovable and admirable," whose goodness causes Huck to tear up his letter telling Jim's owner where to find her runaway slave. By contrast, the "swindlers, members of mobs and feudists" are white. "One might go so far as to say that *Huckleberry Finn* is not fair to white people. It should, nevertheless, be available for use in New York schools." The editorial added: "One is not so certain about the Central High School of Little Rock, Ark."[20]

The *Times* did not explain why it cast doubt on Central High as a place for *Huck Finn;* evidently it considered the point so obvious that no explanation was needed. In retrospect, though, the meaning seems clouded. Was the editorial saying that "one of the deadliest satires" ever written on the "nonsense that goes on with the inequality of races" had no place in a Little Rock school? One doubts that was the intent. Nor does it seem likely that the editors were actually concerned about Twain's presumably unfair treatment of whites; on the other hand, they surely realized there might be a different reaction in Arkansas, which is home to some of *Huck Finn*'s most disreputable and violent characters.[21] In any case, perhaps the editors simply meant to imply that it would be impossible to teach *Huck Finn* at Central High during the eruption, given that the epithet used in the book was also being shouted just outside the classrooms.

Other aspects of the editorial also raise questions. Was it accurate to suggest, as it seems to do, an unequivocal distinction between Little Rock and New York? After all, the epithet that the editors describe as the "Missouri vernacular of that day" was also current, not only in Little Rock but, albeit unsanctioned, nationally. And what exactly was meant by "vernacular"? If "nigger" had been no more than an idiomatic expression in the slaveholding states, at what point did it acquire its contemporary meaning? And why were the editors so certain Mark Twain considered the epithet a mere colloquialism?

In any event, the assertion that the use of "nigger" in *Huck Finn* was merely the vernacular of that time appears to have been an after-the-fact justification. Before desegregation, when white teachers taught the novel exclusively to white students, school officials displayed no curiosity over the students' seeming lack of difficulty with the epithet. But what did the white children really make of it? Had their parents explained it was the rawest, most debasing word in the language? Told them it was a word nice people didn't use? Or provided models for their children by using the epithet themselves? And the teachers? How did they respond to unseemly reactions from students? The public silence ended only when African-American children, having entered schools where they were not wanted, encountered the epithet in the classroom and protested—with predictable results.

"Why is it so obvious to so many authorities that [African-American parents' and students'] complaints cannot be taken seriously?" inquires Arac.[22] Among those who dismiss their objections is a professor of English, Joan DelFattore, who, in 1992, pointed to *Huckleberry Finn*'s "ignorant, hypocritical, and narrow-minded slaveowners" and asserted: "Realistically, what should students think such people would say? 'Invite the African Americans to come in from the fields'?"[23]

If "nigger" were used only by the novel's slaveowners, little comment would be needed. The word is, though, used by almost every character (including black ones), as well as by a narrator who long ago entered our national mythology. That *Huck Finn* is not a book in which the epithet is confined to characters the reader is meant to dislike is reflective of its complexity. The question, though, is not whether Twain should have dispensed with the epithet (he could not have written the novel without it), but whether its ubiquitous use can be justified by one or another historicist or literary defense (as antebellum vernacular, as a synonym for "slave," as Twain's irony).

Blacks have also been derided for their objections to Jim. In what literary historian Donald B. Gibson described in 1968 as a "characteristic" response,[24] Edward Wagenknecht declared: "When Negroes object to Jim . . . one can only regret that they are behaving as stupidly as white folks often do, for surely Jim is one of the noblest characters in American literature."[25] This comment was made in 1961.

More than a decade later, Andrew Solomon asserted: "Though often camouflaged by a minstrel-show exterior, Jim generally gleams through as a sublime creation, and those black readers who are repelled by Jim's external tendencies to stereotype might well ponder . . . Wagenknecht's remark."[26] And a decade after that, Laurence B. Holland spoke of those "skinned in white" in Concord who did not or do not "want their children to know about young Huck Finn," and contemporary "collegians skinned in black who do not see, created in the antics of the Negro Jim, the aspirations of a people and the stature of a man."[27]

Thus, according to these and numerous other critics, the issue was not the black challenges to a black character but the challengers' inability to comprehend what was so obvious to the critics: that Jim is a representative black figure.

IV

The attribution of African Americans' criticisms of *Huck Finn* to a lack of comprehension is accompanied by a seemingly unrelated charge, that the black challengers are "left-wing censors." Among those who make the accusation is DelFattore: "The power of left-wing censors is best illustrated by the treatment of *Huckleberry Finn,* which has become one of the most frequently challenged works taught in secondary schools. Fundamentalists occasionally oppose the novel's portrayal of religion and its glorification of moral independence, but most of its opponents attack its racist language, particularly the word *nigger.*"[28] It would be surprising, not to say distressing, if concern about the effect of "nigger" in the classroom existed only on the Left. If, however, the challenges to the novel are the work of left-wing censors, they can be dismissed as outside interference, of no concern to school officials. No documentation, though, is provided to support the claim, which seems to rest on the silent assumption that black students and parents are incapable of acting on their own.

While the left-wing censors are unnamed, the NAACP has been

one of those so classified. The censorship charge, though, is hardly sustained by the record, which tells us only that the NAACP objected to the "racial slurs" in Mark Twain's works. But if one assumes, despite its denials, that the organization conveyed to the board of education its objections to *Huck Finn* as required reading, one is left with a question: would this act constitute censorship? As for the NAACP's subsequent role, in 1982 it changed its position from objection to praise of *Huck Finn*. However, the organization stressed that the way the novel was taught resulted in the "humiliation" of black children, and it urged that teachers be "trained to handle potentially sensitive areas" before it was placed on required reading lists.[29] Another organization that DelFattore implicitly associates with the censorship charge is the Council on Interracial Books for Children.[30] While the council was sharply critical of *Huckleberry Finn,* it did not oppose the novel's inclusion in the curriculum; instead it offered guidelines for teaching it. The council appears to be inactive.[31] Although there seem to be no national organizations expressing objections to *Huck Finn* as required reading, the protests have continued.

The NAACP's 1957 protest against *Huck Finn*'s "racial slurs" was undoubtedly made in response to complaints from parents. In the following decades, challenges have come from small local groups of parents or individual parents acting on behalf of or with their children, occasionally with the support of school administrators and teachers (including in some instances white ones);[32] in one school, an administrator took the initiative.[33] Scattered and sporadic, the challenges have come from such places as Davenport, Iowa; State College and Warrington, Pennsylvania; Waukegan, Springfield, and Winnetka, Illinois; Deland, Florida; and Houston, Plano, and Lewisville, Texas. (In Lewisville the "Objector" is described as "Student, with his mother.")[34] A challenge has also come from the Pennsylvania State Conference of the NAACP.[35] These protests are met with what Arac calls the "structure of idolatry—that is, the assault by the establishment when African Americans challenge the prestige of *Huckleberry Finn.*" The "standard pattern is for journalists to draw authority from scholars" to put down the parents and children.[36]

V

In 1993, Allen Carey-Webb reported on *Huck Finn*'s status in the schools:

> Praised by our best known critics and writers, the novel is enshrined at the center of the American-literature curriculum. . . . [T]he work is second only to Shakespeare in the frequency with which it appears in the classroom, required in seventy percent of public high schools and seventy-six percent of parochial high schools. The most taught novel, the most taught long work, and the most taught piece of American literature, *Huckleberry Finn* is a staple from junior high (where eleven chapters are included in the Junior Great Books program) to graduate school.[37]

Commenting on why African Americans continue to challenge the novel's use in the classroom, despite seemingly implacable resistance, Carey-Webb states:

> That *Huckleberry Finn* draws the attention of black families should not be a surprise. Since no text by a black—or any other minority group member for that matter—has yet to make it to the list of most frequently taught works, *Huckleberry Finn* has a peculiar visibility. The novel remains the only one in the common "canon" to treat slavery, to represent a black dialect, and to have a significant role for an African American character. The length of the novel, the demands it places on instructional time, and its centrality in the curriculum augment its prominence. Add to this the presence in the novel of the most powerful racial epithet in English—the word appears 213 times—and it is evident why *Huckleberry Finn* legitimately concerns African American parents sending their children into racially mixed classrooms.[38]

If one judges the impact of the challenges to *Huck Finn* by its status in the schools, one could easily dismiss them. They have, though, been felt in less apparent but extremely significant ways. For instance, less than a year after the NAACP protest, support on the question of Jim came from an eminent source. Although he made no mention of the protest, Ralph Ellison stated that when he read *Huck Finn* as a boy, Jim "struck me as a white man's inadequate portrait of a slave." Ellison also linked Jim *in concept* to minstrelsy.[39] Over the years, other authors and critics have extended Ellison's criticisms of Jim, while still others have defended him. Because the debate, as James S. Leonard, editor of the *Mark Twain Circular,* points out, centers on "Jim's intelligence—the most important element necessary for establishing his humanity,"[40] Jim's champions no longer rest their case only on the traditional view of him as kindly, loyal, noble, and so forth. This reading is rivaled by another, which holds that Jim adopts a survival strategy devised by the slaves: deliberately mirroring the stereotypes in white minds, he feigns the traits attributed to him. Whether or not Jim's behavior corresponds to that of the nonfictional slaves is of no small consequence, given that he is known to more readers than any real fugitive slave.

The transformation of the controversy from one over *Huck Finn* and conventional morality to one over *Huck Finn*'s treatment of racial matters has affected the interpretation not only of Jim, but also of Huck, who has been aptly defined as "America's child."[41] Although the designation has been applicable almost since his creation, its meaning has changed. For instance, in the *Atlantic Monthly* in 1897, Charles Miner Thompson, allowing "whiteness" to blot out the ethnicity implied by "Finn," spoke of Huck's "strong and struggling moral nature, so notably Anglo-Saxon."[42] In 1932, Bernard DeVoto continued along the same lines: "Huck speaks to the national shrewdness . . . succeeding by means of native intelligence whose roots are ours—and ours only. In a sense, he exists for a delight or wonder inseparable from the American race."[43] In 1955, one year after the Supreme Court's order on school desegregation, Huck's significance for America underwent a stunning transformation. Lauriat Lane, Jr., wrote: "Starting with the typically American prejudices and easy generalizations about Jim, [Huck] is gradually shocked into an increasingly complex awareness of Jim as a human being. And although Huck's relations with Jim do not so much embody a national attitude as suggest how the nation may purge itself of one, the theme of the Negro is still one which achieves epic stature in *Huckleberry Finn*."[44] Whether Huck overcomes his prejudices, as this and other critics hold, or clings to his original beliefs is a matter of continuing controversy. The answer is of significance for a number of reasons, including its bearing on the Huck-Jim relationship as a legendary black-white friendship.

The long-running debate over *Huck Finn*'s ending (its genesis can be traced to the novel's first American review) has involved not only critics such as Trilling and Leo Marx, but also authors ranging from Ernest Hemingway in the thirties to Toni Morrison in the nineties. Originally centered on literary concerns, the controversy is now focused on the relationship between the ending and racial matters, in particular over whether it engages in racial travesty, or is instead an allegorical condemnation of the racial travesties of the post-Reconstruction era when it was written—an allegory that, as one critic puts it, "satirize[s] the principle and practice of white supremacy."[45]

The controversy around Twain has also changed from one primarily concerned with his personal conflicts to one primarily concerned with his racial attitudes. William Dean Howells was ahead of his time in recognizing that his friend Twain was not free of prejudice. But while Howells acknowledged that racism may have tainted the private Twain, he also maintained that it did not migrate to his work: if Twain's "sense of justice suffered anything of that perversion which so curiously and pitiably maimed the reason of the whole South, it does not appear in his books, where there is not an ungenerous line, but always, on the contrary, a burning resentment of all manner of cruelty and wrong."[46] Now there is debate over the extent to which Twain overcame his early racial attitudes, and whether or to what degree such attitudes affected his work.

While black parents and students have overwhelmingly been critical of *Huck Finn*, black critics have expressed diverse views. This diversity is, though, of a different character from that among white critics. Where only a comparatively small, albeit significant, percentage of the latter give paramount attention to the novel's treatment of racial matters, virtually all African-American critics do so. And despite the diversity of views among black commentators, a far greater proportion of them are critical of *Huck Finn*'s treatment of race than are white ones who deal with this question. Blacks' opinions have also had a profound effect on many white critics and educators. Some of the latter have revised their views of the novel; others may not have greatly altered their opinions, but nonetheless consider the concerns of black parents and students legitimate.

Among the critics who diverge from the expected reaction to the black challenges is the Twain scholar Louis J. Budd, who neither dismisses them as politically inspired nor equates them with the moralists' challenges. Making light of the latter's complaints, he suggests they be dealt with by using "Twain's own best weapon—laughter." However, "charges of racism, when pressed by PTA-committed moderates in the black community, trouble me deeply." The "least that we can do," he concludes, "is to resist the idea that because we have enshrined *Huckleberry Finn* as a classic, it just cannot be racist at times."[47]

No one is, of course, more closely identified with the enshrining of *Huckleberry Finn* than Trilling. True, his view of it as "one of the central documents of American culture" is as germane today as it was when it appeared half a century ago. But the question now—as it was then, although not publicly articulated until African Americans entered the debate—is whether or not the novel subverts "customary beliefs" regarding race. Or given that, as Gates points out, "Race, as a meaningful criterion within the biological sciences, has long been recognized to be a fiction,"[48] the question is: does the novel conflict with or conform to the black, and the white, images in white minds?

We search for the answer by exploring specifics of the novel's treatment of blacks, whites, and relations between them, particularly those between Huck and Jim. This is a demanding task because of the novel's well-known ambiguities, which lend themselves to conflicting readings (passages interpreted by some commentators as antiracist are seen by others as the opposite). We pay special attention to these ambiguities, which arise in particular from the shifting, often elusive connections between Huck's voice and the authorial voice (where does Huck speak for Twain, where is Twain's voice a counterpoint to Huck's?). Our gauge in determining whether—or, rather, *where*—*Huckleberry Finn* subverts or upholds customary beliefs on race is the historical record, chiefly records concerning slaves and masters, but also those concerning free blacks and non-slaveholding whites. These are especially appropriate criteria because the novel is widely assumed to have an authentic, albeit ironic, approach to antebellum times. Our exploration also includes further consideration of the novel's use of the racial epithet; of *Huck Finn* in the classroom; and of the censorship charge.

That a contemporary controversy over a novel dealing with black-white relations during slavery days becomes increasingly intense might seem paradoxical. But the paradox vanishes when one acknowledges the connection between contemporary racial images and attitudes and that not-so-distant past—that is, when one recognizes that the "long encounter of black and white Americans, which began tragically under slavery . . . still proceeds under the long shadow of the plantation."[49]

2   Marginal Boy

I

On the fiftieth anniversary, in 1935, of *Huckleberry Finn*'s publication, F. Scott Fitzgerald wrote, "Huckleberry Finn took the first journey *back*. He was the first to look *back* at the republic from the perspective of the west. His eyes were the first eyes that ever looked at us objectively that were not eyes from overseas. There were mountains at the frontier but he wanted more than mountains to look at with his restive eyes—he wanted to find out about men and how they lived together. And because he turned back we have him forever."[1] Fitzgerald's remarks, with their lyrically imaginative leap that Huck made it to the territory and looked *back,* are clearly evocative. Certainly they evoke an American dream. Not the new arrivals' dream of freedom awaiting at the American shore, but a variant—the dream of Americans who had been here awhile, that freedom (not to mention riches) lay ever further West. In other respects, what the remarks evoke is not as clear as it might once have seemed. How, for instance, should Fitzgerald's "us" be interpreted? Inclusively, or exclusively? Were the first eyes that looked at us objectively actually from overseas? And what of Fitzgerald's belief in Huck's objectivity?

If Huck is objective (as other commentators have also held),[2] he speaks faithfully for an author who can be unequivocally relied upon. In fact, though, *Huckleberry Finn* presents an author-narrator relationship of quite a different kind. That Twain's perspective is antislavery and Huck's is not, and that the concept of racial prejudice, meaningful to Twain, would be meaningless to Huck—these preclude any possibility of a consistently objective narrator. And, too, while Twain often purposefully clouded Huck's "restive eyes" with ideas received from the society Huck lived in, there is, again, the question of the degree to which Twain's own eyes, clear and penetrating as they could be, were not also thus shadowed.

Fitzgerald's remarks also illustrate the role of commentators in creating a legendary Huck. Although some of the myths around *Huck Finn* have not traveled beyond critical circles (for instance, Trilling's myth of Huck as "the servant of the river-god," who "comes very close to being aware of the divine nature of the being he serves"),[3] others occupy a favored place in the national consciousness. One of these is the myth of Huck-the-rebel. It is not that this myth is entirely devoid of truth, but rather that it favors lesser truths over greater ones.

The distinction between Huck as legendary rebel and the Huck that Twain created can already be detected in *The Adventures of Tom Sawyer*. There Twain describes Huck as a "romantic outcast," but even this phrase does not express Twain's own attitude. It is instead that of the properly-brought-up village boys: "everything that goes to make life precious, [Huck] had. So thought every harassed, hampered, respectable boy in St. Petersburg."[4] These boys see a Huck who can come and go as he pleases, is not expected to attend school or church, is free to swear and to fight if he feels like it. Twain, though, allows us to see that it is the boys' vision of Huck that is romantic, not Huck's life: if he can do as he pleases, it is only because his father is the town drunk and his mother dead. So it is not surprising to learn, in *Huckleberry Finn*, that Huck is prone to melancholy, is sometimes so sad he almost wants to die.

If most readers of *Tom Sawyer*, despite Twain's signals to the contrary, see Huck as a rebel, one explanation may be that they have allowed Huck's deeds to eclipse his motives. Take, for instance, Huck's first violation of a taboo in white-black relations. In a passage in *Tom Sawyer* that prefigures Huck's relationship with Jim, Tom asks the homeless boy where he will sleep. Huck replies: "In Ben Rogers's hay-loft. He lets me, and so does his pap's nigger man, Uncle Jake. I tote water for Uncle Jake whenever he wants me to, and any time I ask him he gives me a little something to eat if he can spare it. That's a mighty good nigger, Tom. He likes me, becuz I don't ever act as if I was above him. Sometimes I've set right down and eat *with* him. But you needn't tell that. A body's got to do things when he's awful hungry he wouldn't want to do as a steady thing."⁵ On the one hand, Huck—whom Twain described as a boy with a "sound heart and a deformed conscience"—is humanly appreciative of help from Uncle Jake and reciprocates by giving Uncle Jake what help he can. He is also perceptive enough to recognize that the black man wouldn't like him if he acted as if he were above him. Yet Huck *does* consider him-self above Uncle Jake—not as an objective matter of social station, but because the man is black and Huck is white. (Although Huck never doubts that Uncle Jake, who remains offstage, is taken in by his pretense, a reader may wonder whether an Uncle Jake would not be wary of a white boy who, even in his innermost thoughts, cordons him off as "nigger.")

It was not unusual for the young sons of slaveholders to have a re-lationship with a slave (traditionally known as "Uncle") in which the man would tell the boy stories (Twain himself had such a connection with an "Uncle Dan'l"). Where these boys would go to a black man in search of diversion, Huck goes to Uncle Jake out of need. As a result, the white boy's role is determined by the black man rather than the other way around. But the need that drives Huck to Uncle Jake is also a source of shame, making him do something he "wouldn't want to do as a steady thing." Still, it does not seem that Huck would have any objection to sitting down to eat with Uncle Jake were it not for a mind's eye that looks on censoriously. No incident could better suggest the vast social and emotional distance that separated even the poorest whites from the blacks than this one, which finds Huck—a boy who dresses in rags and sleeps in barrels, whose reputation is so disgraceful that the schoolmaster punishes Tom Sawyer for talking to him—desperate about what people will think if they find out he ate with a black man.⁶

Although Huck's transgression is motivated not by disregard for a taboo but by a need to survive, it may contribute to his rebellious image (one cannot be sure, though, since there seems to be no critical comment on this point). But the image clearly derives, at least in part, from Huck's reaction to his change in circumstances: For all of his life, respectable society has locked him out as the low-down son of a low-down father—a judgment he accepts. But when he and Tom become heroes, and each receives a six-thousand-dollar reward, society reaches out and locks him in. After the Widow Douglas informally adopts him, he makes his first flight from efforts to "sivilize" him (a process he believes to be female-inspired). Huck does not deny that the widow thinks she is being good to him, but she smothers his spirit: "everything's so awful reglar a body can't stand it."[7] Huck's rejection of the regulated life may derive in large part from a child's yearning to be free of adult restrictions, but it resonates beyond: by resisting an alien notion of how his life should be lived, by his resentment against conforming to regulation, by dreaming of how he might escape, he has become emblematic.

But Huck's desire to escape being civilized also has its own contrarieties, given that his yearning to be outside is not entirely free of a wish to be inside. This conflict is first suggested in *Tom Sawyer:* after Huck runs away from the widow, Tom finds him and says that Huck cannot join Tom's gang of robbers "if you ain't respectable." A desperate Huck pleads: "You wouldn't shet me out, would you, Tom? You wouldn't do that, now, *would* you, Tom?"[8] That Huck must be respectable to join a gang of robbers is the comic mask hiding the threat of ostracism, a deceptively humorous way of saying that sanction equals right. Yet after being coerced into respectability, Huck does not entirely disdain the perquisites that accompany it. In *Huckleberry Finn,* after spending some months in the widow's home, he acknowledges, "I liked the old ways best, but I was getting so I liked the new ones, too, a little bit."[9] Still, the benefits civilization may offer Huck are never matched by what it demands in return. As Tom Quirk observes, Huck accepts "the world's judgment upon him," but he "never fully accepts the world's corrections or refusals of him."[10]

At the beginning of *Huckleberry Finn*, when the runaway Huck returns to the widow's home, he is again confronted with the kind of situation that made him light out: the new clothes that make him sweat; the widow's readings from the Bible, including "Moses and the Bulrushers"; her little hypocrisies (she calls Huck's smoking a mean practice but thinks it all right to take snuff "because she done it herself" [chap. 1]). And now her "old maid" sister Miss Watson has come to stay. Although these passages may make it appear that *Huck Finn* simply picks up where *Tom Sawyer* leaves off, immediate differences are apparent—one of which adds a new dimension to Huck's rebel image.

In *Tom Sawyer*, we learn that authority figures do not like Huck's ways and that Huck cannot bear his life in the home of one of them. But now he also exhibits a certain skepticism toward these figures. "As a general rule, he remains unpersuaded by the words of the authority figures he meets," notes Peter Messent.[11] Often the words and deeds of these figures lead Huck to take action, usually covert, that conflicts with their agendas and enhances his aura of rebelliousness (even though defiance is not his motive). This aura persists despite the fact that the author's social outlook conflicts with that of his narrator. As Toni Morrison points out, "On this young, but streetsmart innocent," Twain "inscribes a critique of slavery."[12] By violating his unknowing narrator's point of view, Twain inscribes his critique and, at the same time, marks the boundaries of his narrator's dissent from authority. Such passages as the following illustrate the point:

When Huck yawns and stretches against the deadly dullness of an evening with the sisters, Miss Watson "pecks" relentlessly at him. Convinced of his incorrigibility, she tells him about "the bad place." When he says "I wished I was there," she gets angry, but he assures readers he meant no harm: "All I wanted was a change, I warn't particular. She said it was wicked to say what I said . . . *she* was going to live so as to go to the good place. Well, I couldn't see no advantage in going where she was going, so I made up my mind I wouldn't try for it" (chap. 1). On one level, the virtually humorless Huck is simply describing thoughts that are logical to him but sacrilegious to Miss

Watson; on another level, Twain satirizes a slaveholder who proclaims she is living so as to go to the "good place."

In another passage, Huck is informed by Miss Watson that prayer will bring whatever he asks for. After repeated prayers bring no more than a fishline without hooks, Huck confronts the widow with his failed experiment. When she tells him that prayers bring "spiritual gifts," he says, "This was too many for me, but she told me what she meant—I must help other people, and do everything I could for other people, and look out for them all the time, and never think about myself. . . . [B]ut I couldn't see no advantage about it—except for the other people" (chap. 3).

Literal-minded though he may be, Huck's questioning of the widow's explanation—a skepticism that cuts through virtuous cant and brings him to an iconoclastic conclusion—places a certain distance between him and society's expectation that its precepts will be honored. Of course, there is no connection between his conclusion and Twain's oblique message about a slaveowner who says she thinks only of the welfare of other people, who reads to Huck from the Bible, oblivious that she is attempting to inspire him with reverence for an infant who grows up to lead his people out of slavery.

Early in the novel, Twain also inscribes his critique of slavery on his unaware narrator in another way: after Huck, with palpable intensity, tells how dull an evening with the two sisters is, how lonesome he feels, his tone abruptly becomes neutral, detached—that is, changes to one appropriate for relating an ordinary, everyday detail: "By and by they fetched the niggers in and had prayers, and then everybody was off to bed" (chap. 1). Thus the Huck who is so quick to see hypocrisy in the widow's forbidding him to smoke when she herself takes snuff is also the Huck who sees nothing hypocritical in slaveowners calling in their slaves for religious instruction. That he spots the minute hypocrisy and is blind to the gargantuan one suggests how ordinary, how *natural*, slavery may have appeared to whites who lived amidst it all their lives. The "horror of slavery was its absolute domesticity," observes Hortense J. Spillers. So "complete was its articulation with the domestic economy that from one angle it loses visibility and becomes . . . 'natural' to the dynamics of culture."[13]

At the same time that Twain inscribes an antislavery critique on his narrator, he also distracts from it. Though Huck is an unreliable narrator, he may be considered dependable when it comes to the widow and Miss Watson, at least if we conceive of dependability as agreement between what the narrator sees and what the author expects the reader to see. Everything Huck says coincides with what a reader in the nineteenth century, a time when a (white) woman was defined by her marital status, would be expected to think of a widow and a woman who never married. If the widow is kindly toward Huck, it is because she was once chosen by a man and lived with him as his wife. If Miss Watson is harsh with Huck, it is because she was rejected by men, is ignorant of their ways, and bitter at them. Later, the sisters enact their widow and old-maid roles once again: when Miss Watson wants to sell Jim, the widow tries to stop her. That these two characters are slaveowners and also invested with traits supposedly peculiar to females makes them the object of two incompatible types of humor: one is aimed subtly at hypocritical slaveowners, the other bids us to laugh reflexively at a foolish widow and a mean old maid.

Huck's rebellion against what he perceives as constraints imposed by women is an ironic one, since the real-life counterparts of *Huck Finn*'s female slaveholders occupied an odd, dual status: they were economic beneficiaries of the slave system, while they were consigned by the men of their world to social subordination.

II

After prayers, Huck goes up to his room. Downstairs, as the boy sitting in judgment on the adults, he felt alone; upstairs, he *is* alone. Downstairs, he felt lonesome; now he feels so lonesome he wishes he were dead. The night forest is not pressed between two hard covers; it is outside his window. Without the women who intrude into his private life, but whose intrusions are also a distraction, he is overcome by fears and apprehension. Birds and animals, familiar by daylight, become prophets of death and mourners of those already dead, while ghosts are made restless by messages they are unable to deliver. When he unthinkingly flicks a spider off his shoulder, it falls into a candle flame. The burnt-up insect is so powerful an omen of ill-fortune that it renders countersigns useless. The supernatural, Huck's only means of coping with unknown dangers, has turned on him, multiplying his fears.

A remarkable departure from the traditional use of superstition for comic effect at a character's expense, this passage has multiple implications. It suggests the narrator's vulnerability, as well as his foreboding. Not only are dislocation and violence among the few things he can count on, but, we soon learn, he fears that his supposedly dead father is still alive. The passage also suggests the social conditions that engender superstition: the natural phenomena interpreted as bad omens by the barely schooled boy coincide with his preexisting fears—thus implying a relationship between a negligible store of formal knowledge and susceptibility to notions of the supernatural.

At the moment he is depressed, but his spirits will revive when, at midnight, Tom Sawyer arrives and Huck slips out the window to meet him. In doing so, he rebuffs the widow's strictures; again, though, his motivation is not defiance, but a need to locate a space where he can feel free, easy, and comfortable. That he finds it unbearable for the sisters to tell him what to do, while also finding it perfectly natural for them to dictate the every move of black adults, contrasts unsettlingly with the image of Huck as rebel.

Commenting on Twain's description of Huck as a boy with "a sound heart and a deformed conscience," Henry Nash Smith states: "Huck's conscience is simply the attitudes he has taken over from his environment. What is still sound in him is an impulse from the deepest level of his personality that struggles against the overlay of prejudice . . . imposed on all members of the society."[14] If his attitudes toward blacks—let alone those of the society as a whole—are merely an "overlay of prejudice," Huck's sound impulse at the deepest level will surely triumph over his prejudice. If, though, prejudice has seeped down to the level of sound impulse, the latter will, at the very least, have an uphill battle.

3 ┃ Shifting Perspectives

I

When Huck climbs out of the window at midnight to meet Tom who waits below, they are at one with their image as "*the* American boys of legend. More than any other characters in our literature, they represent some fabled, delicious freedom of boyhood," observed Alfred Kazin.[1] If the connection between the legend and what the boys do that night is murky, it may be that myths, like caricatures, take one or another feature and exaggerate it, reducing what surrounds it to insignificance.

As the boys sneak away from the house, Huck trips and they learn they are not alone: "Miss Watson's big nigger, named Jim, was setting in the kitchen door; we could see him pretty clear, because there was a light behind him" (chap. 2). Jim, who has been awakened by the noise, demands to be told who is there; when he gets no answer, he declares he will sit there until he hears the noise again; minutes later he falls asleep, snoring loudly. Tom decides to play a trick.

Among the many distinctions blurred by the myths around *Huckleberry Finn* and *Tom Sawyer* is that between the Tom of the earlier book and the Tom of the later one. There may be a greater connection, though, between the two Toms than is immediately apparent. If, say, readers with memories of Tom as delightful prankster revisit the legendary whitewashing incident, they may not find it quite the innocent fun of memory; when Tom tricks his friends into paying for the privilege of painting the fence, he is, after all, the little con man playing the other boys for suckers. Still, he displays such an imaginative grasp of his friends' psychology that the incident, even when reconsidered, is engaging, particularly since the other boys get such satisfaction from doing the painting. That is, the incident is engaging if one overlooks its prelude, which has not entered our national memory.

That prototypical summer day begins as Tom, ordered to do the painting, is about to see the "free boys . . . come tripping along on all sorts of delicious expeditions."[2] But "free boys" may be interpreted in more than one way, since there is also a boy who enters and exits before Tom's friends appear. A slave (also) named Jim, the boy is owned by Aunt Polly (the whereabouts of his mother and father is a question lurking beneath the surface of the shimmering summer day). Jim is not on a delicious expedition. He is on his way to the town pump, a chore Tom ordinarily finds hateful; today he tries to lure Jim into switching chores. "Ole missis she'd take an' tar de head off'n me," retorts Jim to "Mars Tom," who scoffingly insists that Aunt Polly never hurts anyone.[3]

Jim succumbs to Tom's lures ("Jim was only human," Twain reminds, or informs, his young readers); a moment later he is "flying down the street with . . . a tingling rear," while Aunt Polly departs "with a slipper in her hand and triumph in her eye."[4] Tom, the culprit, is unscathed. Although Aunt Polly's punishment of Jim, compared to that actually given to slaves, is negligible, it differs from her punishment of white boys, on whom she never inflicts pain. But such nuances give way before a giddy Jim, who skips and sings "Buffalo Gals," a variation on a song from minstrelsy.[5] Thus it is quite easy for readers to overlook the shadow the black boy casts over the legendary day and on Tom, who does not hesitate to take advantage of the boy's unfree condition for his own ends.

In *Huckleberry Finn*, Tom has in mind a trick of a different order from the one he played on his friends. It is reflective of a society where "Negro hunting, Negro catching, Negro watching and Negro whipping constituted the favorite sport of many youthful whites."[6]

Tom wants to tie Jim to a tree, a trick whose special cruelty arises both from the fact that the designated victim is already in bondage and that masters tie up their slaves to whip them. Huck disapproves of the trick for his own reasons; it could wake Jim, who might "make a disturbance, and then they'd find out I warn't in" (chap. 2). Tom substitutes another trick, one that, if successful, will demonstrate his psychological control over a black man.

II

Huck's remark that "we could see [Jim] pretty clear, because there was a light behind him" seems no more than straightforward description. Mary Kemp Davis reminds us, though, why *Huck Finn* is renowned for its ambiguities: "What Huck and Tom Sawyer see is not Jim at all but his silhouette; Jim is enveloped in darkness, his hulking frame thrown into relief by the light at his back. This seemingly naturalistic detail foreshadows Huck's later association with Jim when he slowly discovers that much of Jim's identity is concealed behind a mask of blackness."[7] Thus Davis uses a striking metaphor to express her view of Huck's relationship with Jim. Her remarks, though, also raise questions. *Does* Huck embark on a voyage of discovery of Jim's identity? What, in fact, *is* Jim's identity? How great is the difference between him and his two-dimensional silhouette? Does he have the traits whites ascribe to blacks, or does he himself put on a "mask of blackness"—that is, deliberately conform to stereotype—to keep whites from seeing him? These questions inevitably suggest another: if Huck makes discoveries about Jim, what effect do they have on Huck?

When Davis speaks of Huck's "later association with Jim," she is clearly referring to the relationship between the runaway boy and the runaway slave that begins on Jackson's Island. However, before dealing with their subsequent association, let us consider the preliminaries, starting with Jim's reaction to Tom's trick. According to the tale Jim tells, the witches put him in a trance, rode him through the state, set him back under the trees, and hung his hat on a limb. Jim embellishes his tale with each telling, with the witches eventually riding him all over the world, tiring him "most to death." Jim is so "monstrous proud," says Huck, that he hardly notices the other slaves, who "would come miles" to hear his tale. "He was more looked up to than any nigger in that country. Strange niggers would stand with their mouths open and look him all over, same as if he was a wonder." Jim wears a five-cent piece (it was left in the kitchen by Tom to pay for candles) that he says is a charm given him by the devil. "Jim was most ruined, for a servant, because he got so stuck up on account of having seen the devil and been rode by witches" (chap. 2).

Critical reaction to this episode has undergone acute changes. In 1932, Bernard DeVoto, who saw Jim as a member of a "child-like race of slaves," wrote: "That [Huck] survived the menace of the unseen world was due wholly to Jim, a Negro, who was expert in manipulating it."[8] In 1963, Chadwick Hansen, identifying the Jim of this scene as a "comic stage Negro," observed that readers are given implicit permission to laugh at him: "His essential quality in this particular case is that he feels no humiliation as a result of Tom's trick. His ignorance protects him from the mental pain of humiliation. . . . [S]ince he does not suffer we are free to laugh at the incongruity between his account of the event and the reality."[9]

In 1984, Fredrick Woodard and Donnarae MacCann, taking the witch-trick incident as an illustration, held that the black characters in *Huckleberry Finn* conform to minstrelsy's depiction of blacks: Jim, as well as the other blacks, are "not used to poke fun at white attitudes about Black people; Jim is portrayed as a kindly comic who *does* act foolishly."[10] Woodard and MacCann's assessment has evoked counterarguments.

In 1984, David L. Smith maintained that while Jim may seem to adhere to the black stereotype, he actually subverts it: "Twain uses Jim's superstition to make points which undermine rather than revalidate the dominant racial discourse." Jim, Smith holds, displays rhetorical skills, creates a narrative in which he is the hero, and wins the admiration of the other slaves. Smith points to Huck's remark that Jim was "most ruined, for a servant" as evidence that Jim's owner, not Jim, suffers from the hoax because of a decrease in his unpaid labor.[11] In 1988, Forrest G. Robinson offered a corresponding view, arguing that Huck and Tom, because of their prior assumption of Jim's gullibility, fail to recognize that Jim benefits from the hoax. Robinson also finds confirmation of Jim's success in Huck's "ruined, for a servant" remark, which he sees as "perfectly unconscious irony."[12]

Huck's remark is indeed ironic, but not because Jim's involuntary labor decreases; since Jim tells his tale at unspecified hours, there is no basis for assuming his performances occur during work-time (he later says that until his escape he went off with the cattle each day about dawn). Huck's words are ironic because they are those of a poor white boy echoing the slaveowners, who asserted that anything from "lenient" treatment to the proximity of abolitionists would "ruin" slaves.[13]

In 1992, Shelley Fisher Fishkin, writing in support of Smith's view, also took issue with Woodard and MacCann: given Twain's "fondness for minstrel shows," it may be assumed that "some minstrel material worked its way into the novel," but "to assume that . . . this material necessarily comes from minstrel routines . . . is to deny that Twain had access to other sources." If Jim's tale is seen within the context of African-American folktales, with which Twain was familiar, his "'superstitiousness' and 'gullibility' about having been taken on a late-night ride by a supernatural being take on a different meaning." To support her contention that Jim's tale may have come out of the black folk tradition, Fishkin cites similarities between his tale and those collected in Gladys-Marie Fry's *Night Riders in Black Folk History*.[14] But this approach raises a question: do similarities necessarily imply affinities? Consider first the circumstances in which the slaves created their tales:

To control their slaves' movements, particularly at night, the masters used brutal patrollers. However, according to African-American oral history, the masters also attempted to exert psychological control over their slaves by spreading rumors that supernatural beings roamed the plantations at night. To give seeming substance to the rumors, slaveowners and overseers masqueraded as ghosts.[15] This control strategy, Fry points out, was based on the simplistic assumption that because a belief in supernatural phenomena was widespread among the slaves, the slaves would believe the masters' tales of terrifying supernatural beings. What the masters failed to grasp was that the slaves "not only believed in ghosts and other supernatural phenomena, but also realized that deception was being practiced by the whites." Thus, while the strategy created fear, it was "not so much fear of unknown ghosts as it was of known whites."[16]

One of the ways that the slaves coped with their owners' efforts at psychological control was to create tales in which a slave sees something supernatural that chases him until he is exhausted, but who then overcomes overwhelming odds to win out against his adversary. Thus, although there is a parallel (as Fishkin points out) between Jim's being chased by a supernatural being until he is "tired most to death," there are essential differences. In the slaves' tales, the pursuers do not catch the narrator, who becomes an object of admiration by winning against all odds. By contrast, Jim becomes an object of admiration to the other slaves even though the witches render him instantly helpless. Further, although humor is the "dominant tone" of the folktales,[17] the tale told by Jim—who, unlike his creator, is oblivious to deadpan humor—is comic neither to him nor to his slave listeners. Hence, the young-master figure who perpetrated the hoax can laugh not only at Jim but at the other blacks as well.

There are also striking differences in the conditions under which the slaves told their tales and Jim tells his tale. While the masters used patrollers and supposed supernatural beings to control their slaves' activity, Jim and his black listeners appear to face no constrictions, given that the latter "would come miles" to hear him. The words "would come" signify that these gatherings are a repeated phenomenon, with blacks who are unknown in the area ("strange niggers," in Huck's words) freely moving from their masters' places to wherever Jim holds forth. That Jim and his listeners gather openly at unspecified times—unconcerned with passes, masters, or patrollers—implies benign owners who permit their slaves to roam at will. In reality, in 1823 Missouri—fearful of slave plots and insurrections—authorized its counties to set up patrols to prevent slaves from going anywhere without their masters' consent. Further, as a means of preventing unlawful assemblies of slaves, the patrollers were empowered to enter the quarters and lash the inhabitants.[18]

Tales of night riders not only helped the slaves contend with an oppressive reality, but were also inspired by reality, that is, by the ways in which slaves outmaneuvered both the disguised night riders (one slave recognized his mistress masquerading as a ghost, and threw rocks)[19] and the undisguised ones: the blacks tripped the patrollers' horses with grapevines or ropes, posted lookouts who warned the slaves and misled the patrollers, wore cowbells at night, and presented out-of-date passes to patrollers who could not read.[20]

III

Huck's description of Jim as "monstrous proud" and "stuck up" reflects his glee at Jim's reactions to the hoax. Although his glee may seem paradoxical, given that he himself is in thrall to superstition, this is not necessarily the case: even if he had not been in on the hoax, he surely knows he would not have been taken in. He turns to the supernatural to protect himself or predict the future, but he also makes commonsense distinctions, as do superstitious people in general. As Fry observes, "The universal acceptance of the supernatural has long been recognized as the 'common heritage of humanity.'"[21] But when Jim fails to connect his hat's new location with the decidedly earthly noises that awakened him, the fact that blacks are the favorite targets of white-boy tricks, and the probable proximity of Huck and Tom, his gullibility denies this common heritage, thus preserving the belief that blacks have a singular proclivity for superstition.

Although the Jim of the hoax episode is, as Hansen notes, a "comic stage Negro," those who laugh at him do not see him as such; they laugh because they believe he is authentic. Their reactions are analogous to those of Huck, who is gleeful because Jim's behavior and that of the other blacks is just what he expects. Thus when he goes to his initial face-to-face encounter with Jim, his assumption of superiority as a white has, it would seem to him, been confirmed.

Huck, aware that Pap has come back and is after his son's money, has given his six thousand dollars to Judge Thatcher (the judge, insisting that legal niceties be observed, gives Huck a dollar for "*sell[ing]* all your property to me" [chap. 4]). Desperate to learn what

Pap is up to, Huck seeks out Jim, who tells fortunes by listening to the spirit in a hairball. Sometimes, he says, it won't talk without money. Huck decides to say nothing about the dollar the judge gave him, and offers the hairball a patently counterfeit quarter. (Evidently, a big sum of money is an abstraction to Huck, but a small one that can easily be converted into things he may want is real.) When Jim says he knows a trick with a raw potato that will transform the coin so it will pass for the real thing, Huck leaps to assure his readers, "I knowed a potato would do that, before, but I had forgot it" (chap. 4).

Although Jim gets the better of Huck, a larger question lingers: does he get the better of the comic-Negro stereotype? Contending that he does, Robinson describes the incident as the first of a series in which "racist self-deception" is accompanied by "openings for manipulation by the seemingly hapless, in fact shrewdly resourceful, victims."[22] In defining the Jim of the hairball incident as shrewdly resourceful, Robinson places him in the company of the slaves who outwitted their masters. That Jim's adversary is a white boy rather than a white adult is a significant change in the original cast, but even this is not decisive. The essential point is that Jim does not best the boy by demonstrating adult wit or mature consciousness, but by knowing a little trick.

That Jim knows the trick and Huck does not is of no significance; it is Huck's reaction—that of a white boy who cannot bear for a black man to outdo him—that makes him the loser. Robinson says as much: "By insisting that he forgot what in fact he never knew, the boy submerges the awkward revelation that the tables have been turned on him. Such an acknowledgment so conflicts with the racist prepossessions manifest in his attempt to deceive Jim that he cannot rise to it."[23] At the same time that this is an acute assessment of Huck's mentality, it overlooks—or rather rejects—that Huck, having seen Jim's behavior during the hoax incident, has reason to assume he will be gullible enough to accept the fake coin.

IV

When Huck returns to his room that night, Pap is there. Pap of the rags and caved-in hat. Pap, whose eyes shine from behind tangled, greasy hair as if through long black vines. Pap, whose white skin is, in Huck's words, "not like another man's white, but a white to make a body sick, a white to make a body's flesh crawl—a tree-toad white, a fish-belly white" (chap. 5). Pap has come for his son's money. Furious when he cannot get his hands on it, he soon kidnaps Huck and takes him to a cabin in the woods. Huck finds existence there to his liking, except for Pap's beatings. The father's violence climaxes on the night he delivers a racist tirade and then, in a fit of delirium tremens, takes Huck for the Angel of Death and tries to knife him. To escape from Pap, Huck stages his own murder; he shoots a pig, hacks its throat, and pulls out his own hair to leave on the bloodied axe.

Soon there will be the failed search for Huck's body, with his presumed death followed by his rebirth in numerous guises. The open question is, then, whether the Huck who starts down the river is transformed, if not by his rebirth, by his journey with a fugitive slave.

<table>
<tr><td>4</td><td>Black Roots,

White Roots</td></tr>
</table>

I

As *Huckleberry Finn*'s genealogy has slowly been brought to light, some antecedents—including Southwestern humor, Northeastern humorists, and the picaresque novel—have been enthusiastically acknowledged. But certain other forebears have met with a generally chilly reception. This was the case with Ellison's revelation of the novel's connections with minstrelsy. It has also been true of the revelations, in the 1980s, of its links with fugitive slave narratives.

When Fitzgerald said that Huck's "eyes were the first eyes that ever looked at us objectively that were not eyes from overseas," he was undoubtedly referring to European eyes. He did not say what these eyes saw, but a famous European critic scorned not only the roughness, rudeness, and vulgarity in the United States, but indicted the hypocrisy in a nation that professed democracy and practiced slavery.[1] Europeans were not, however, the first to see Euro-Americans objectively. Among those who preceded them were Africans and African Americans, whose objectivity, uncompromised by preconceptions of dark-skinned peoples, is recorded in a variety of forms, including the slave narratives, which were first published in the latter part of the eighteenth century.

In the decades before the Civil War, slave narratives were bestsellers. *The Interesting Narratives of the Life of Olaudah Equiano* (1789) had gone through thirty-six editions by 1850.[2] By 1847, two years after its publication, nine editions of the *Narrative of the Life of Frederick Douglass* had been printed. And *Twelve Years a Slave; Narrative of Solomon Northup* (1853) sold twenty-seven thousand copies in its first two years. "Black autobiography had a mass impact on the conscience of antebellum Americans," states William L. Andrews.[3]

That the autobiographies had such an impact can be traced to two interrelated factors. One was the rising protest against slavery, the other the narrators' success in carrying out their dual objectives: to reveal slavery's horrors and to demonstrate the disparity between the slaves and the stereotypes created of them. "The narrators wanted (and their African American readers expected them) to correct, complete, or challenge . . . stereotypes and the half-truths," points out Frances Smith Foster.[4]

A particularly significant gauge of the narratives' impact is the ferocity of the counterattack from the slaveowners and their sympathizers, who denounced the narratives as inauthentic.[5] By the end of Reconstruction, the counteroffensive had virtually destroyed the slaves' antebellum testimony. "The stilling of the black 'voice' assumed myriad forms, not the least distressing of which was the effective destruction of black arts and letters existing before 1865," state Charles T. Davis and Henry Louis Gates. Many decades were to pass before scholars could even begin to restore "the fragments of the lost records of the Afro-American mind."[6]

During the time the narratives were effectively destroyed, attacks against them continued. In the first decades of the twentieth century, they were dismissed by historians who justified their rejection with a "pernicious double-standard, finding 'bias' in the slave's text and 'objectivity' in that of the master," Davis and Gates note.[7] The pivotal figure in dismissing the narratives as biased was Ulrich B. Phillips, who was also instrumental in perpetuating the myth of the happy slave: "a courteous acceptance of subordination" and "a readiness for loyalty of a feudal sort" were, he held, among the slave's distinguishing traits.[8] In making these claims, Phillips ignored evidence he was surely aware of—including the descriptions masters most frequently gave in advertising for runaways: "humble," "inoffensive," and "cheerful." "Slaves such as these apparently concealed their feelings and behaved as they were expected to—until one day they suddenly made off," states Kenneth Stampp.[9]

Commenting, in 1842, on those who saw the slaves not as they were but as they wanted them to be, the fugitive Lewis Clarke declared: "Some have thought their slaves were so much attached to them, that nobody could coax them away; and them very slaves now reside in Canada. Others think the slaves are too brutified to think or care anything about freedom; and them's the worst deceived of all."[10] Escaped slaves, having learned while in captivity to make use of the masters' proclivity for self-deception, were well prepared for their new roles. "Fugitive slaves honed the art of pretense into a sharp-edged tool of self-defense," notes Gilbert Osofsky.[11]

The art of pretense was simply a manifestation of a remarkable resourcefulness. Male fugitives pretended to be women, female fugitives to be men. Literate runaways wrote their own passes; nonliterate ones paid poor whites to write passes for them. Fugitives covered their arms and legs with red pepper, or put dust from graves on their bodies to throw off bloodhounds tracking a human scent. A fugitive nailed himself up in a box and shipped himself to freedom. Another tied himself to the underside of a train. Fugitives stowed away in the holds of North-bound ships, often with the help of black sailors or friendly white captains. Fugitives feigned loyalty and submission, but when their masters took them to the North, they vanished. Some runaways asked whites for directions and then went the other way. Their "greatest enem[y]" was the white man. "If the slave was surprised by an ignorant white man, he flashed any piece of paper with writing on it in front of his face and usually succeeded in deceiving his adversary. When accosted by a white man he could not deceive, he ran. If cornered, he sometimes fought and killed his pursuers," relates John Blassingame.[12]

Although the antebellum slave narratives had vanished from general attention before *Huckleberry Finn* was written, Twain was well acquainted with them. "Slave narratives . . . inspired Twain throughout his career. . . . The presence of slave narratives in Twain's library, references to them in his letters and conversations, and echoes, in his fiction, of some of their characteristic incidents or strategies suggest a rich familiarity and strong interest on Twain's part," states Twain scholar Fishkin.[13]

The account with which *Huck Finn* has the broadest connections is the *Narrative of William Wells Brown* (1847), which was also a best-seller. "The river, the boats, the hiding by day and sneaking by night . . . Brown's narrative is a definitive prototype for Mark Twain's treatment of these issues," Lucinda MacKethan observes.[14] A number of other parallels also support her conclusion: Brown and his mother escaped in a stolen skiff, the means by which Jim first hopes to escape. The mother and son's starting point was St. Louis, which Huck and Jim pass near the beginning of their voyage ("The fifth night we passed St. Louis, and it was like the whole world lit up" [chap. 12]). Brown and his mother made their way, as Jim first plans to do, to the Illinois shore. They hid in the woods by day and traveled on foot at night; on the eleventh day of their flight, they were caught. Brown's mother was sold down the river; they never saw each other again. Brown was eventually sold to the owner of a boat; he established himself in the eyes of his master as a loyal slave, and waited for his chance. The boat's first docking in a free state was at Cairo, Illinois, where Jim hopes to gain his freedom.[15]

At the same time that there are parallels between Brown's *Narrative* and *Huckleberry Finn,* there are also profound differences—not simply the differences between an autobiography and a novel, but distinctions arising from the novel's roots in antithetical traditions.

II

While Brown's narrative and those of other fugitive slaves challenged stereotypes, powerful forces—not only the slaveowners, but scientists, philosophers, statesmen, historians, and religious and cultural figures—perpetuated them. And not only did the black challengers have to compete with influential whites speaking as authorities on blacks; they also had to contend with influential whites speaking *as* blacks: the minstrels, who used the mask of blackface as a "space of habitation" for "that deep-seated denial of the indisputable humanity of inhabitants of and descendants from the continent of Africa," states Houston A. Baker, Jr.[16]

Well before the American Revolution, white performers smeared with burnt cork appeared on stage, giving the stereotypes that arose with slavery an animated, vocal presence. By the 1830s, the minstrel shows began their rise to prominence and soon dominated nineteenth-century entertainment. Minstrelsy "codif[ied] the public image of blacks as the prototypical Fool or Sambo," states Mel Watkins.[17] To turn those held in bondage into the nation's comic relief, the minstrels stole and distorted elements of African-American culture. "The fact that white minstrels may have gathered African-American material for their shows did not prevent them from transforming that material into productions that demeaned blacks in the nineteenth century, and whose legacy continues to plague African Americans to this day," comments Fishkin.[18]

While the slave narratives stirred white consciences, the blackface minstrels anesthetized them. "Minstrelsy not only conveyed explicit pro-slavery and anti-Abolitionist propaganda; it was, in and of itself, a defense of slavery because its main content stemmed from the myth of the benign plantation," states Alexander Saxton. According to the myth, "Slaves loved the master. They dreaded freedom because, presumably, they were incapable of *self*-possession. When forced to leave the plantation they longed only to return."[19] Minstrelsy also included fugitive slaves among those who yearned for plantation life: they ended up as "repentant runaways," points out Robert C. Toll.[20]

Twain, who left a record of his interest in the slave narratives, also left evidence of his devotion to minstrelsy.[21] His melding in *Huck Finn* of these contentious elements begins in the scenes on Jackson's Island: Huck, who is lonely after a few days there, is delighted when he catches sight of Jim. Jim, who has heard that Huck was murdered, stares at him wildly, gets down on his knees and pleads with the boy not to hurt him, assuring Huck he has always liked dead people and always been his friend. Jim is soon convinced that Huck is alive, but reacts anew when Huck brings in provisions he has kept in the canoe. "The nigger was set back considerable, because he reckoned it was all done with witchcraft" (chap. 8).

Jim's minstrel-like behavior and Huck's contemptuous response, variants of their behavior in earlier scenes, soon give way to a different kind of exchange. After Huck tells Jim why he is on the island and asks him to do the same, Jim responds warily:

> "Maybe I better not tell."
> "Why, Jim?"
> "Well, dey's reasons. But you wouldn' tell on me ef I 'uz to tell you, would you, Huck?"
> "Blamed if I would, Jim."
> "Well, I b'lieve you, Huck. I—I *run off.*"
> "Jim!"

Jim—quick to note that Huck's "Jim!" is less an expression of surprise than a shocked reprimand—reminds Huck that he has promised not to tell.

> "Well, I did. I said I wouldn't, and I'll stick to it. Honest *injun* I will. People would call me a low down Ablitionist and despise me for keeping mum—but that don't make no difference. I ain't agoing to tell, and I ain't agoing back there anyways." (Chap. 8)

If Jim can take comfort from anything Huck has said, it is certainly not his boyish promise to keep mum, but that he "ain't agoing back there anyways." In any event, Jim has little immediate choice but to try to keep the boy—who has been taught to demonize abolitionists, but wants to hear how a slave escaped—more or less friendly. And so Jim tells his story: Miss Watson has promised never to sell him, but he notices that a "nigger trader" keeps coming by. Late one night, an alert Jim—the inverse of the Jim who goes back to sleep after unexplained noises awaken him—steals into the house and hears Miss Watson tell the widow that she cannot resist the eight hundred dollars offered for her slave. "I lit out mighty quick, I tell you," Jim says (chap. 8). Still, before lighting out, he coolly estimates that the two sisters, who are to leave early the next morning for a camp meeting, will think he has gone off with the cattle.

Jim hides out, concealing himself for a day under wood shavings. He plans to steal a skiff, but they are all being used to hunt for Huck's body. Jim reevaluates: if he keeps going on foot, dogs will track him; if he steals a skiff, its owners will miss it. Only a raft will do, because it "doan' *make* no track" (chap. 8). He climbs aboard one, calculates that given the strength of the current, he will be twenty-five miles downstream before dawn, where he plans to swim to the Illinois shore. Faced with the danger of discovery, he slides overboard and swims to Jackson's Island.

Jim's tale is that of a slave who confounds the stereotype and a slaveowner who falls victim to it. Had Miss Watson not believed that blacks lack powers of perception, she would not have behaved so carelessly, allowing a slavetrader into her home and then divulging information she means to keep secret. Jim, by contrast, is bold, resourceful, visualizing actions and reactions, even displaying the mathematical ability blacks are supposedly devoid of. And unlike minstrelsy's blacks, Jim never becomes a repentant runaway; instead of longing for his owner and the old plantation (so to speak), he longs for freedom and mourns for his family. And far from hating abolitionists, he plans to have one "steal" his wife and children.

There is also a hint that Jim has thoughts he keeps from Huck. Soon after the two meet, Jim exclaims, "But you got a gun, hain't you?" The remark seems perfectly natural, given that Jim, who has been living off the island's vegetation, connects the gun to hunting. However, just after Jim tells how he escaped, he repeats the gun refrain: "But you got a gun. Oh, yes, you got a gun" (chap. 8). While Jim again connects the gun to game, he has to be aware that Huck, as a white male, is legally authorized to bring in fugitive slaves. There is no hint, though, that he even considers getting the gun—an essential for a fugitive slave[22]—away from Huck and escaping in the canoe.

But such speculation gives way to a larger question: why, during the days before he encounters Huck, does Jim not even consider trying to reach his original objective, the Illinois shore, which is only a quarter of a mile away? Addressing this perplexing matter, Sculley Bradley asked: "What is to prevent Jim from later crossing that short space to free soil? By Illinois law, Negroes without freedom papers were subject to arrest and indentured labor. But the risks of going down river into slave territory seem greater still."[23] When Bradley says there is no reason why Jim could not have crossed over "later," he is apparently countering the argument that Jim could not cross over to Illinois because slavehunters would likely be after him near the scene of his escape. But perilous as Illinois may be, it is hopeless for Jim to stay on the island. While slavehunters may be looking for him just across the river (and also much further down, as they did with Brown and his mother), they come after him on Jackson's Island.[24]

Just what is it that prevents Jim from crossing over to Illinois? Bradley replies: "One answer is that, given the geography, Clemens's narrative would have stalled at the outset without this disguised improbability. Readers forget in the controversy over the ending how skillfully Clemens's art makes them suspend disbelief in the beginning."[25] The reader's acceptance of Jim's anomalous behavior is not left, though, only to a willingness to suspend disbelief. There is a textual justification for his inaction: a change in attitude toward his escape once he reaches Jackson's Island. Although he has to be well aware that slavehunters will be looking for him there, the thought does not seem to bother him: "I had my pipe en a plug er dog-leg, en some matches in my cap, en dey warn't wet, so I 'uz all right" (chap. 8). That Jim suddenly veers from a quick-thinking fugitive bent on freedom to a fugitive unconcerned with his perilous situation and content with ephemeral comforts would be inexplicable were it not for his roots in blackface minstrelsy as well as the fugitive slave narratives. Moreover, even in those instances where Jim's remarks have an affinity with the latter tradition, his speech is a reminder of his conflicting roots: his "voice retains enough of minstrelsy in it to be demeaning and depressing," observes Fishkin.[26]

That Jim is an amalgam of antagonistic traditions can be seen not only in obvious contrarieties, but also in more subtle ways. Take the matter of trust. "It seems likely that [fugitive slaves] seldom trusted anyone but fellow slaves. A few white Southerners who opposed slavery gave sanctuary to fugitives or directed them along their routes," states Stampp.[27] But Jim does not trust his fellow slaves; in making his plans to escape, he seems to have considered them a threat: "De yuther servants wouldn' miss me, kase dey'd shin out en take holiday, soon as de ole folks 'uz out'n de way" (chap. 8). Still, since there were slaves who betrayed other slaves, Jim could have had reason to slip secretly away (although none for deriding his fellow slaves for avoiding involuntary labor when they are left, oddly enough, without supervision). On the other hand, Jim's approach to Huck is less easily explained.

In contrast to fugitives who knew enough about certain rare Southern whites to trust them, Jim knows enough about Huck not to trust him. In fact, Jim simultaneously seems to distrust Huck and want to keep Huck with him. In acting on the latter feeling, Jim shows that he, too, has "honed the art of pretense into a sharp-edged tool of self-defense"—or, to be exact, what Jim, as an alloy of antithetical traditions, conceives as self-defense.

The first time Jim appears to practice the art of pretense is in a cavern, where he and Huck take shelter after Jim's sign-reading predicts a storm. Huck, eating fish and hot cornbread, exclaims: "I wouldn't want to be nowhere else but here." Clearly the boy, who has momentarily achieved his ideal of freedom and comfort, has no notion of how his remark would sound to a fugitive slave trapped in slave territory. Without commenting on his own feelings, Jim retorts that, without Jim, "You'd a ben down dah in de woods widout any dinner, en gittn' mos' drownded, too, dat you would, honey" (chap. 9). If Jim's concern is simply what it appears to be, keeping "honey" snug and well fed, he would fit neatly into the "mammy" convention. His real concern, though, is keeping Huck with him. Jim's ability to maneuver the unaware white boy into staying by his side is antistereotypical, but it also raises a question: is there a match between Jim's stratagem and his objective? Consider the following incident:

Huck and Jim, paddling around the island after the river overflows, come upon a floating house; they see what looks like a man lying in a far corner. Jim hollers at him (it is singular that he would try to rouse a man whose color he cannot make out). After deciding the man is dead, Jim goes in; he discovers the man has been shot to death and, before Huck enters, instructs the boy not to look at the face ("it's too gashly" [chap. 9]). Not until the novel's end, when Jim learns he has been freed, does he tell Huck the dead man was his father.

Why does Jim withhold the man's identity? In the view of a number of critics, he does so to protect Huck, or, as Robert Sattelmeyer puts it, to protect Huck "from the shock of seeing the corpse of his debauched father."[28] But if this were Jim's motive, why would he not warn Huck against looking at the ghastly face, and tell him some time after they leave that the man was his father? Another critic, Louis D. Rubin, Jr., divined that Jim has a different reason for withholding the news, and—after pointing out that Huck is not trying to help Jim escape, but fleeing from his father—rebuked him: "Should not Jim have told him that [his father is dead]?" Does he fail to do so partly because he "knows that he will need Huck's help if he is ever to make his way to freedom"?[29] Still another critic, Jeffrey Steinbrink, held that although it was unlikely, if Huck *were* to return to St. Petersburg, Jim would have "good reason to fear that Huck might inform on him." But he also considered the threat of betrayal insufficient reason for Jim to withhold the news: "We might expect the 'better' Jim . . . to waste no time in sharing the 'comfortable' news of Pap's death, whatever the personal consequences."[30]

So, according to these views, Jim is noble if he tells Huck the news of Pap's death to comfort him or withholds the news to protect him, but Jim is selfish if he withholds it to protect himself. The moral universe of *Huck Finn*, though, allows us to see Jim's deception in a different way—that is, as analogous to Huck's famous "moral lies": where Huck lies to protect Jim, Jim deceives Huck to protect his own escape and his chances of rescuing his family.

In this instance, then, there is a match between Jim's stratagem to keep Huck with him and his objective of escaping to free territory. A different question is raised, though, by the assertion that Jim "knows that he will need Huck's help" to make his way to freedom. Why does Jim know—or, rather, believe—that his escape requires Huck's help? If Jim believes this, as he surely does, it can only be for one of two reasons: that, in the minstrel tradition, he is dependent upon whites; or, conversely, that he has reason to believe Huck will help or at least can be manipulated into providing help.

That Jim succeeds in concealing Pap's death from Huck may make him feel that he can control the boy. The authorial voice, however, hints that Jim has misjudged. For instance, when Huck and Jim leave the floating house, it is almost broad daylight. "I made Jim lay down in the canoe and cover up with the quilt, because if he set up, people could tell he was a nigger a good ways off" (chap. 9). Does Jim, a man who hid himself under wood shavings for an entire day, have to be told to conceal himself—or does he have a reason for wanting to see where they are headed? And although his sole expressed concern is that Jim may be seen *from a distance* if he sits up, Huck not only has Jim lie down, he also has Jim cover up with a quilt. After thus making sure that Jim cannot see where they are going, Huck paddles over to the Illinois shore.

Huck's aversion to connecting Jim with free soil, albeit not yet necessarily conscious, is also revealed in a little story he tells: a catfish as big as a man bites a hook he and Jim have put out. "We couldn't handle him, of course; he would a flung us into Illinois," says Huck (chap. 10), overlooking that Jim would regard a fish that did this as a providential transport. Huck also demonstrates his untrustworthiness by playing a trick on Jim. Not long after he has derided Jim for warning that snakeskins bring bad luck, Huck kills a rattlesnake, curls it up on Jim's blanket, and looks forward to "some fun." Huck then forgets about the dead snake; he also forgets the folk belief that a live snake returns to its dead mate. That night the presumed mate bites Jim. Huck kills it, as Jim grabs Pap's whiskey jug and begins to "pour it down," until, finally, he gets drunk. He is laid up for days. Huck gets rid of the two snakes that would divulge his guilt to Jim. He also atones for disregarding Jim's warning about snakeskins by promising himself never to touch one again—as if trying to convince the reader, as well as himself, that touching the snakeskin was his real misdeed. Jim suspects nothing (chap. 10).

Huck also has other qualities, including his whims, that make him a dubious companion for a fugitive slave. When the bored and restless boy wants to go back to town to find out "what was going on" (chap. 10), surprisingly Jim encourages him—even though he should already know what is going on: that slavehunters are surely after him and, instead of tarrying on the island, he should long since have tried to get away. When Huck returns, he gives his famous order: "Git up and hump yourself, Jim! There ain't a minute to lose. They're after us!" (chap. 11).[31]

To be sure, "they" are not after "us"; they are after Jim. Still, if they catch Jim, they will also catch Huck and return him to a civilization that will surely punish him for consorting with an escaped slave. But beyond these literal meanings, there may also be other meanings: instead of jettisoning Jim, Huck seems to identify with him. And even if he has not faced up to the fact that Jim is a runaway, Huck does not want the slavehunters to catch him. So, however circumscribed his intent, Huck's "They're after us!" ignores the constraints that split "us" at the color line. At the same time, though, if they are after "us," Huck is entitled to a say in shaping the escape strategy. That he has, in fact, already left his mark on it may be divined from what he tells about their plans: instead of making an immediate dash for the Illinois shore, they will do so only if a boat should come along. Since they forget to put a gun, a fishline, or any provisions in the canoe, it is a good thing, observes the master provisioner of his own escape, that no boat comes.

So, unlike those rare white Southerners who "directed [fugitive slaves] along their routes," Huck inadvertently reveals that if he can, he will—without malice aforethought, or any thought at all, really—alter Jim's route. Huck's attitude is both unconsciously ironic and perfectly authentic for a boy who has been led to believe slavery is sacrosanct. As for Jim, we could expect him to react with a consistent awareness, ironic or otherwise, of what the white boy is up to, if his roots were not split between two antithetical traditions.

<table>
<tr><td>5</td><td>Shallows, Depths,
and Crosscurrents</td></tr>
</table>

I

Huck and Jim, river and raft. Huck and Jim, floating down the river on their raft. The images are so familiar that it is easy to mistake familiarity for accessibility. In reality, the mythology they evoke is not easy to decipher, given that it identifies legendary black-white amity and unbounded, dreamlike freedom with a voyage that takes a fugitive slave ever further south. By and large, critics have overlooked this paradox; in fact, a recurring interpretation of the raft interludes absorbs the myth and elaborates on it in distinctive ways.

For instance: "Huck describes his harmony with Jim and with the natural world. . . . They light up their pipes, dangle their legs in the water, and talk 'about all kinds of things—we was always naked, day and night, whenever the mosquitoes would let us.' They shed the clothes that symbolize the Grangerfords' civilization," states Robert Shulman.[1] Lauriat Lane shifts the symbolism from the clothes to the nakedness: "The nakedness of Huck and Jim when they are alone on the raft becomes a symbol of how they have shucked off the excrescences of the real world, their clothes, and have come as close as possible to the world of the spirit."[2] The implication that skin color ceases to matter when the two are away from civilization—that they spontaneously move beyond color consciousness and see in each other only a color-free humanity—is made explicit by a third critic:

Huck's and Jim's roles are those of "free man and black man, master and slave," but when they are stripped of their clothes on the river, the relationship between them is that of "two men . . . without the mediating vision of society to dictate their behavior," states Michael J. Hoffman.[3]

That the text does not justify the view that skin color loses its significance when Huck and Jim are alone on the raft is not to say there is no difference between raft life and shore life in this respect. On the contrary, so long as Huck and Jim are alone, they so casually transgress the color line—the two never talk about their living arrangements, they simply enter into them—that a black and a white sharing quarters, sharing their daily lives, seems perfectly normal in a society where it is a crime. That Huck's way of life defies society does not necessarily imply, however, that he believes society is wrong. Nor does the breaching of the color line on the raft transcend the direction of the voyage.

II

"Goodness sakes, would a runaway nigger run *south?*" exclaims Huck (chap. 20), in an effort to turn back a menacing inquiry into Jim's status. Huck's retort is a quick-witted way of coping with a threat, but it also has a side effect: it casts a glaring, if glancing, light on the question that hovers over *Huckleberry Finn* from the time Jim becomes aware that they passed Cairo in the fog.

If Huck's response momentarily seems to accentuate a problem, it also has other implications: by having his narrator use an incongruity to protect Jim, Twain makes a virtue of a paradox—or, to put it another way, he daringly confronts the paradox and then ignores it. Although critics as a whole have taken Twain's implicit advice and overlooked the incongruity, not all have done so. "The downstream movement of the story . . . runs counter to Jim's effort to escape. Life on the raft may indeed be read as implied criticism of civilization—but it doesn't get Jim any closer to freedom," declared William Van O'Connor in 1955.[4]

It is not possible, of course, to differ with O'Connor on this point.

A number of critics have, though, attempted to explain, along the following lines, why Twain sent a fugitive slave south: Twain knew the Mississippi River but not the Ohio, and the direction of the voyage allowed him to comment on lower Mississippi Valley shore life.[5] But these explanations, while seeming to answer the question, actually raised another: if Twain's only major concern had been to portray Southern whites, why did he go to so much trouble to keep Jim in the picture? Toni Morrison provides an answer: "There is no way, given the confines of the novel, for Huck to mature into a moral human being *in America* without Jim. To let Jim go free, to let him enter the mouth of the Ohio River and pass into free territory, would be to abandon the whole premise of the book. Neither Huck nor Mark Twain can tolerate, in imaginative terms, Jim freed. That would blast the predilection from its mooring."[6]

In deciding to send Jim in a reverse direction, Twain must have felt confident that his readers would find the reversal believable.[7] Since the various mishaps he supplies to justify the southerly direction (fog, loss of the canoe, etc.) are exhausted early on, he clearly did not rely on these alone to ensure his readers' acceptance of the inversion. Whether or not he gave the matter conscious thought, that acceptance depended on their perception of Jim, that is, on whether they would accept him as a fugitive slave who *would* go south. Ensuring this was not a problem, really: so pervasive were racial stereotypes—in particular as conveyed through minstrelsy—that most whites were preconditioned to believe no behavior too illogical for a black.

Although *Huck Finn's* early readers lived in minstrelsy's time, they probably did not notice—given that minstrelsy had blurred their ability to distinguish between blacks and blackface[8]—that its influence on the novel is both implicit and quite explicit. For instance, a dialogue on Jackson's Island is not only minstrel-like in substance, but follows minstrelsy in form: Huck plays an interlocutor and Jim an endman (the endmen mocked the interlocutor's pomposity, but he was definitively presented as their superior).[9] The exchange begins when Huck, who has heard Jim display a copious knowledge of bad-luck omens, asks if he knows any good-luck signs. After Jim thinks of one—a hairy breast, denoting riches to come—Huck, with sly logic and a coolly superior air, inquires:

> "Have you got hairy arms and a hairy breast, Jim?"
> "What's de use to ax dat question? don' you see I has?"
> "Well, are you rich?"

Jim replies that he was rich once.

> "Wunst I had foteen dollars, but I tuck to specalat'n', en got busted out."
> "What did you speculate in, Jim?"
> "Well, fust I tackled stock."
> "What kind of stock?"
> "Why, live stock. Cattle, you know." (Chap. 8)

Jim's obliviousness, on the one hand, that "stock" has more than one meaning, and his use, on the other, of "specalat'n'" as it would be used on Wall Street, spring from a minstrel convention that portrayed blacks as ludicrous imitators of highly placed whites.[10]

In his other minstrel-type exchanges with Jim, Huck descends from the role of interlocutor to that of an endman quarreling with another endman. And, far from anyone's gaze but Jim's, he reveals acute anxiety lest it not be continually evident that he, as a white, is the smarter. One such dispute begins after he reads to Jim from a book about royalty. When Jim says Solomon is the only king he ever heard of, Huck instructs him about kings: "everything belongs to them." "*Ain'* dat gay?" responds Jim. Huck also tells Jim that Solomon had a harem of "about a million wives." Previously unfamiliar with the word, Jim likens a harem to a boardinghouse and derides the belief that Solomon was wise: a wise man wouldn't have lived amidst the "blimblammin'" of quarreling wives, he would have built a boiler factory that could be shut down. Huck asserts that Solomon *was* the wisest man, citing the Widow Douglas as his authority. Jim retorts that he doesn't care what the widow says, and asks if Huck knows about the child Solomon was "gwyne to chop in two." Huck still insists Jim has missed the point. "Blame de pint!" Jim exclaims, declaring the *"real* pint is down furder—it's down deeper": a man with one or two children values them, but a man with "'bout five million chillen" would as soon chop up a child as a cat (chap. 14).

Jim's aversion to Solomon's behavior, some critics note, prefigures the love he later expresses for his own children. Neil Schmitz sees added implications in Jim's antipathy: "The real point *is* 'down deeper.' Jim has instinctively recognized in Solomon the figure of the slaveholder, the white Southerner who regards the Negro as chattel. He speaks from the depths of his own experience about the 'chile er two' that 'warn't no consekens to Sollermun,' his own children—all the black families dismembered on the block."[11] There are suggestions that Jim does see Solomon in this way.

When Jim disdains the widow's opinion of Solomon, he engages in an open denial of white authority. And though his seeming unawareness of the traditional belief that Solomon never intended to cut the baby in two may weaken his argument rhetorically, it does not rob it of merit; as an enslaved person, he has good reason to believe verbal threats translate into physical ones. "No risk had existed prior to his threat, but through the action of language, Solomon introduced danger, and whatever his intention, the effect is the same. Fake threats, in other words, become real by virtue of contexts," Lee Clark Mitchell observes.[12]

But other aspects of Jim's reaction cast doubt on the contention that he connects Solomon with the slavemasters. When Huck says that kings own everything, Jim's response (*"Ain'* dat gay?") is curiously giddy. And while Jim condemns Solomon's attitude toward his children, he does not question Solomon's treatment of their mothers. Expressing misogynous sentiments that accord with those of certain literary comedians of a later day, Jim portrays Solomon as the victim of quarrelsome women, not the women as victims of a tyrannical, licentious man.[13] And since "harem" was used in the antebellum South to suggest the nature of the master's relations with his female slaves,[14] Jim's use of the word as a synonym for boardinghouse desexualizes the harem (as well as himself) and signals that he is grotesquely naive as to what masters imposed on black women. And, too, Jim's argument that the more children a man has the less he values them is dubious when applied to an ordinary man, but specious when applied to the slaveowner, who valued his children not according to their quantity but their color. Because he placed one value on his children by his white wife and another on his children by his slaves, the families he dismembered on the auction block often included his own sons and daughters.[15]

After Jim refuses to back down on Solomon, Huck converts him into an unworthy adversary ("I never see such a nigger. If he got a notion in his head once, there warn't no getting it out again" [chap. 14]). Reverting to his preferred role as mentor, Huck tells Jim about French royalty. When Jim hears that Frenchmen speak French, he is dumbfounded. Huck argues that since it is "natural and right" for cats and cows to "talk" differently from each other and differently from "*us,*" it is "natural and right for a *Frenchman* to talk different from us." Jim asks Huck if a cat or a cow is a man, or a cow a cat.

> "No, she ain't either of them."
> "Well, den! she ain' got no business to talk like either one er the yuther of 'em. Is a Frenchman a man?"
> "Yes."
> "*Well,* den! Dad blame it, why doan he *talk* like a man?—you answer me *dat!*"
> I see it warn't no use wasting words—you can't learn a nigger to argue. (Chap. 14)

Contention over this passage was set off when Woodard and MacCann declared that while "Jim is the more logical," the "debate 'plays' like the dialogue in a minstrel show because Jim has the information base of a child (*i.e.,* Jim believes English to be the world's only language)."[16] In a rebuttal, Steven Mailloux dismisses Jim's lack of knowledge: "Far from demonstrating Jim's inferior knowledge, the debate dramatizes his argumentative superiority, and in doing so makes a serious ideological point through a rhetoric of humor."[17]

Perhaps the debate could be considered a serious ideological exercise via a rhetoric of humor if Jim's score for logic is divorced from the rest of his performance. In context, though, his supposed victory can be seen as part of a convoluted joke. The joke's starting point is Jim's comical information base. The joke continues when the newly literate Huck tries to argue along formal logical lines. Another facet is added when Jim—who, like Huck, thinks animals "talk"—catches Huck in his categorical confusion of men with animals. Jim's points for logic, already qualified by his own confusion of species, are further reduced by the syllogism that lurks within his next lines: men speak English, Frenchmen are men, therefore Frenchmen speak English. The syllogism—which invites the reader to laugh at a Jim who may have learned to argue, but whose argument is ludicrous—reiterates the dialogue's false premise: that an African-American slave would believe a single language exists.

"The notion that the Middle Passage was so traumatic that it functioned to create in the African a tabula rasa of consciousness is as odd as it is a fiction, a fiction that has served several economic orders and their attendant ideologies," declares Gates.[18] Jim's consciousness is just such a tabula rasa. He believes everyone speaks the same language, even though an African-American slave would have heard Africans speak their own languages or, at the very least, words that Africans added to English or to one of the other languages they acquired in this country. (When Douglass was a slave in Maryland around 1830, the other slaves mixed words from so many African languages with English that "I could scarcely understand them when I first went among them.")[19] It is also ironic that Jim is astounded to hear that men speak French: during the period that would roughly correspond with his early years, Missouri, as part of the Louisiana territory, was under French control.[20]

Nor does Jim display any interest in expanding his minute information base. When Huck reads to him, there is no hint that he would like to learn to read—a reaction that sets him apart from the slaves of history, whose desire for literacy was often so intense that they learned to read at the risk of severe punishment.[21]

Despite the artificiality of the episode, Huck's authenticity is (dismaying as this may be) enhanced. When he can read to Jim and inform (or misinform) him about the world, he is expansive; when he thinks Jim gets the better of him, his sensibilities are roiled. Although he has previously rejected the widow's interpretation of biblical stories, he retreats across the color line and uses her presumed authority to squelch Jim. And he considers it "right and natural" to include Jim among "*us*" until he fears he has lost the argument and spitefully shoves Jim back into the "nigger" slot.

III

In his debates with Jim, Huck's resentment appears to reflect a generic racism rather than a special animus toward his companion. However, at a less than conscious level, there is the basis for a more personal antagonism: a submerged dread that when they get to Cairo, Jim will escape to free soil and he will have been an accomplice to Jim's crime.

Huck's inner resentment begins to surface after a swift current and a "solid white fog" separate him from Jim. Huck, who is in the canoe, lets out whoops and hears answering ones, but is unable to determine where they come from. "I did wish the fool would think to beat a tin pan," complains Huck. But since the whoops, Huck tells us, may be coming from another raftsman, Jim's failure to beat a tin pan may arise from the fear that if he does so, a white stranger will reach him before Huck does. Finally deciding that Jim has drowned, Huck expresses no regret and goes to sleep. When he wakes, he sees Jim asleep on the raft. Huck climbs aboard, lies down, and mimes a person waking from a deep sleep. After Jim ecstatically greets the boy he believed dead ("It's too good for true, honey, it's too good for true"), Huck launches into a skillfully malicious interrogation. No doubt remembering how much whiskey it took before Jim got drunk enough to numb the snakebite pain, Pap's son demands: "What's the matter with you, Jim? You been a drinking?" Jim comically, not to say stereotypically, gives Huck the satisfaction he is after: "Has I ben a drinkin'? Has I had a chance to be a drinkin'?" (chap. 15).

Huck calls Jim to his face what he thought of him when they were apart ("tangle-headed old fool"), and methodically denies ("What fog?") Jim's account of the events leading up to their separation. Huck insists that Jim was dreaming, and finally Jim agrees. At Huck's behest, he describes his "dream," "'terprets" what the current and the whoops "stood for," and concludes with a message: if they avoid aggravating "all kinds of mean folks," they will reach the "big, clear river," the free states. Huck points to a broken oar and the debris washed on board, and asks what *they* stand for. It takes time for Jim to overcome the illusion that reality was a dream, but finally he looks at Huck "without ever smiling," and says:

> "What do dey stan' for? I's gwyne to tell you. When I got all wore out wid work, en wid de callin' for you, en went to sleep, my heart wuz mos' broke bekase you wuz los', en I didn' k'yer no mo' what become er me en de raf'. En when I wake up en fine you back agin, all safe en soun', de tears come en I could a got down on my knees en kiss' yo' foot I's so thankful. En all you wuz thinkin 'bout wuz how you could make a fool uv ole Jim wid a lie. Dat truck dah is *trash;* en trash is what people is dat puts dirt on de head er day fren's en makes 'em ashamed." (Chap. 15)

So a mask is lifted and a semi-stranger steps out to tell the poor white boy that he *is* just what he has been known as all his life. That Jim could not only say this but say it "without ever smiling" would, just moments before, have been unimaginable to Huck.

In this stinging rebuke to Huck for his invasion of human dignity, Jim says that people who put dirt on their friends' heads make their friends ashamed. Ashamed, yes, but of whom? The ones who make fools of them? Or themselves for having been made fools of? Or both? In this passage, Jim uses ambiguity, dual meaning, and metaphor to such effect that one wonders why he is so easy to fool, so gullible that he suspects nothing until the prankster taunts him with the truth. One may wonder, too, why Jim, a man with a family, would say he did not care what happened to him when he believed Huck was lost. And it is also curious that at the same time he puts Huck in his place, he stays in his own presumed place by projecting a servile self-image ("I could a got down on my knees en kiss' yo' foot").

While the clash between stereotype and human characteristics produces incongruities in Jim, the clash between human impulse and social conditioning adds depth to Huck:

> It made me feel so mean I could almost kissed *his* foot to get him to take it back.
>
> It was fifteen minutes before I could work myself up to go and humble myself to a nigger—but I done it, and I warn't ever sorry for it afterwards, neither. I didn't do him no more mean tricks, and I wouldn't done that one if I'd a knowed it would make him feel that way. (Chap. 15)

Huck has learned, he says, that Jim can feel bad, which, he also says, is something he didn't know before. We need not doubt that he believes this, nor should we doubt that, at some deep level, he knows it is not true. His remorse, though, is not in doubt. Still, remorseful as he is, he does not cede a centimeter of his social identity. Huck may be trash, but he is still *white* trash; so, where Jim says he could have kissed Huck's foot, Huck preserves his racial distance by saying he could "almost" have kissed Jim's foot. Nor should Huck's statement that he would not have played the trick if he had known it would make Jim "feel that way" be taken literally. "Huck knew the trick would humiliate Jim; that was the point of playing it. What he did not anticipate was that Jim would respond . . . with a sharp, dignified rebuke," notes Robinson.[22]

It is tempting to interpret "solid white fog" as a metaphor for Huck's state of mind, but in reality the fog that clouds his perceptions of blacks is not dense enough to shield him fully, as Rhett Jones has pointed out, from the knowledge that blacks are human.[23] The glimmers and flashes of truth that seep through leave his mind reeling, reeling to the point where he can say he never regretted "humbl[ing] myself to a nigger." But while his lack of regret for his apology suggests growth, he also sees himself, even in retrospect, as apologizing not to Jim but "humbling" himself to a "nigger." Whether this means that "nigger" prevails in his mind over the humanity he recognizes in Jim, or that the epithet cannot hide the humanity of the people it is applied to—or both—would be hard to say. In any event, when Huck describes his apology to Jim as an act of abasement, he overlooks that, after apologizing, he felt himself lifted out of a morass of meanness.

6   Identity Crisis

I

In *Huckleberry Finn,* slavery seems fixed, permanent, while everything else is in flux, transitory. Identities mutate as if in a dream, or nightmare. Hallucinatory as these shifting personae may seem, their roots can be traced to a time when it was quite simple for white males to pick up, move on, and reappear with different names and histories. Included among those who stealthily relocated were debt-ridden slaveowners who escaped in the night from one state to another, bringing their slaves, as well as new or revised identities, with them.[1]

Huck, who forever picks up and moves on, is a master creator of identities. Although his personae proliferate, they are all variations on a single theme: the simultaneous creation and destruction of families. Psychologically orphaned before he learns the facts, he fantasizes families that invert the American dream in its Horatio Alger mode: his families do not aim to strike it rich but, at most, attempt to escape complete destitution. Failing even at that, they go from poor to poorer, then die. Although Huck thus plays a continually changing cast of characters, the identities he creates suggest a constant self-image.

The same cannot be said of Jim, whose loss of identity as a fugitive slave—or, to put it another way, as a human being confronted with a particular set of circumstances—becomes increasingly pronounced as the raft drifts downstream. Take the next plan for his escape. It calls, Huck tells us, for them to sell the raft at Cairo, get on a steamboat, and go up the Ohio "amongst the free States" (chap. 15). Jim's belief that he will be able to buy a ticket and board a steamboat is an extension of his illusion that he will be safe when he reaches Cairo. Had he considered the realities, he would have been concerned as to how a black man without identification papers might avoid the slavehunters. The impossible plan evaporates when they pass Cairo in the fog.

At one point, though, Jim again briefly conforms to the identity of a fugitive slave. When he and Huck believe they are approaching Cairo, he is beside himself with joy. Huck is beside himself for other reasons. Where Jim feels "all over trembly and feverish to be so close to freedom," Huck feels the same sensations "because I begun to get it through my head that he *was* most free—and who was to blame for it? Why, *me*." His conscience comes calling in various guises, including that of "poor Miss Watson," Jim's "rightful" owner. When Jim says he will work to buy his wife and if necessary get an abolitionist to "steal" his children, Huck's inner voice echoes the master's: Jim would never have dared talk that way before; the old saying is right, "give a nigger an inch and he'll take an ell."[2] When Jim is sure they have finally reached Cairo ("We's safe, Huck, we's safe! Jump up and crack yo' heels, dat's de good ole Cairo at las', I jis knows it!"), Huck's secret hope emerges as cool reason; he will take the canoe and find out if it really is Cairo since it "mightn't be, you know" (chap. 16).

As Jim reveals his innermost thoughts, he seems unaware that Huck's silence conceals unspeakable ones. But as Huck shoves off to "tell," Jim says he'll soon be shouting for joy and he owes it all to Huck, the best friend he ever had, the *only* friend he has now. Jim's words follow Huck over the water, elevating the white-trash boy to "quality," praising the would-be Judas for his nobility: "Dah you goes, de ole true Huck; de on'y white genlman dat ever kep' his promise to ole Jim." Huck feels sick but decides "I *got* to do it" (chap. 16).[3]

Before he can reach the shore, Huck meets slavehunters, who demand to know whether there is a white or a black man on the raft. Try as he might, he is unable to tell them the truth ("I warn't man enough—hadn't the spunk of a rabbit"). When they say they will see for themselves if the man is white, Huck encourages them, telling them his family is sick and needs help. When he avoids naming the malady ("it ain't anything, much"), they become frantic. After they advise Huck on how to lie so people will not guess that his family has smallpox, their consciences, inert when they go after their black quarry, come guiltily alive; they leave forty dollars in gold for a white family in need. Huck splits the money with Jim (chap. 16).

William Andrews has traced the genesis of this remarkable episode, which presents Huck with his first crisis of conscience, to a slave narrative, *The Fugitive Blacksmith; or, Events in the History of James W. C. Pennington, Pastor of a Presbyterian Church, New York, Formerly a Slave in the State of Maryland, United States* (1849). Attempting to escape through the Maryland countryside, Pennington was captured by a large group of white men. When they demanded the name of his owner, he told a bold and brilliant lie: he was part of a gang of slaves being taken to Georgia by a slavetrader; the trader fell sick and died of smallpox, as did several of the slaves. "No one claimed us, or wished to have anything to do with us," Pennington informed his captors. He soon perceived signs of panic; some of the men moved to a "respectful distance," others moved even further away, murmuring "better let the small-pox nigger go." Pennington was left in the custody of one man, whom he eluded in a race across a field.[4]

Andrews shows that the parallel between *Huck Finn*'s treatment of the smallpox lie and that in *The Fugitive Blacksmith* goes beyond the lie itself to "similarities of substance, tone, and thematic purpose." For both Pennington and Huck, the lie is an occasion for intense self-searching: "Though successful in evading exterior pursuers, neither runaway can escape the judgments of his conscience."[5] Pennington, whose parents raised him to be truthful, put the matter as follows: "If you ask me if I expected when I left home to gain my liberty by fabrications and untruths? I answer, No!" If Pennington did not applaud himself on outwitting his captors, neither did he castigate himself for violating his parents' strictures. Instead he expressed the "most intense horror at a system which can put a man not only in peril of liberty, limb, and life itself, but which may even send him in haste to the bar of God with a lie upon his lips."[6] Huck's soul-searching takes him on a different route; he places the onus for his lie on a parent who valued lies as much as Pennington's parents valued the truth: "a body that don't get *started* right when he's little, ain't got no show" (chap. 16).[7] Thus, Andrews points out, Huck's lie "represents an act of rebellion by [his] heart in defiance of his society-trained conscience."[8]

At the same time that Andrews's essay reveals Twain's mastery in adapting the incident to fit Huck, it also implicitly raises a question: how does the adaptation affect Jim? Clearly, the transposition of the smallpox lie from a black man to a white boy is of great significance. The transfer need not have been definitive, though, if Jim otherwise acted as the agent of his own escape. But the fact that Huck lies to protect Jim, while Jim waits on the sidelines as his fate is decided by whites, is emblematic. To be sure, Jim's manipulation of Huck prevents Huck from betraying him; but where Jim maneuvers the boy by appealing to his heart, the boy outmaneuvers slavehunters. Further, while Pennington beats seemingly insuperable odds by outwitting whites *after* they capture him, Jim succumbs to superstition and gives up after Huck *prevents* his capture: when he realizes they have passed Cairo, Jim—now transmuted into the voice of all blacks—declares, "Po' niggers can't have no luck. I awluz 'spected dat rattle-snake skin warn't done wid its work" (chap. 16). That Jim, believing himself the victim of supernatural forces, renounces the struggle for his own freedom is evident. That he has lost all touch with reality does not, however, become fully apparent until the next episode.

The transition to this sequence occurs when a steamboat crashes through the raft and Huck and Jim are separated. Huck calls for Jim, but hears no answer. Thinking he has drowned, Huck heads for shore, where he is taken in by Colonel Grangerford, owner of one hundred slaves. In one of his first utterances, the colonel demands: "Betsy, you old fool—ain't you got any sense?" (chap. 17). Were she not a slave, Betsy might well have turned the question back to the questioner—the father who leads his sons in a chivalric dance of death. Huck is drawn to the youngest son, Buck, who has been initiated into the Grangerford-Shepherdson feud, and is also well versed in his role as young master. "Each person had their own nigger to wait on them," says Huck. "My nigger had a monstrous easy time, because I warn't used to having anybody do anything for me, but Buck's was on the jump most of the time" (chap. 18). That an adult black must act on the dictates of a white child hints that the laws sanctioning the Grangerfords' way of life are far more terrible than the lawlessness of their feud, which is, after all, elective, if insane, violence between peer groups.

The terror with which the Grangerfords maintain their lifestyle is reflected in Jim's situation; he is hiding in a swamp on or near the Grangerford place, where the water keeps him from the Grangerford dogs. "By jings it was my old Jim!" exclaims Huck, again revealing the ease with which poor whites acquired the master's mentality. Jim, who has arranged for Huck to learn of his whereabouts, almost cries with delight when he sees Huck. He tells Huck that the other blacks showed him this hiding place and bring him food. "Dey's mighty good to me, dese niggers is, en whatever I wants 'm to do fur me, I doan' have to ast 'm twice, honey" (chap. 18). Jim conveys an accurate portrait of the slave community's solidarity with fugitives,[9] but one doubts that it would have been forthcoming in his case. If other slaves learned that a fugitive was heading South, they would surely have considered his behavior so bizarre as to bring his sanity into question—not to mention their own safety, particularly if they also learn that his escape is being conducted under the aegis of a white boy staying with their master.

Up until this episode, Jim's going South has been portrayed as the result of one mishap after another. But now his behavior becomes willfully antithetical to that of a fugitive slave: when he fears that Huck has been killed in the feud's bloody climax, he is all set to continue South on the raft by himself. Not only would one expect a rational Jim to try to head North, he now has a uniquely favorable opportunity to do so: with no Grangerford males left to maintain control, the place would likely be in turmoil, offering a propitious moment for the Grangerford slaves to do what real slaves often did— help steer a fugitive slave North. (It also seems likely that at least some of the slaves would have taken advantage of the situation to try to escape.)

When Huck leaves Jim in the swamp, he says nothing about

seeing him again; clearly he is enjoying himself too much at the Grangerfords' to think of leaving. It is only after the carnage that he is sickened and wants to get away. Of their return to the river, Huck remarks: "We said there warn't no home like a raft, after all. Other places do seem so cramped up and smothery, but a raft don't. You feel mighty free and easy and comfortable on a raft" (chap. 18). So Huck depicts raft life—as he and Jim travel ever further South, following a route once described as "southward to that (for the colored man) Valley of the Shadow of Death, where the Mississippi sweeps along."[10]

II

Jim is silent about raft life. But however one might expect his perceptions to differ from Huck's, his existence is surely idyllic compared to what it becomes when the two con men, the king/dauphin and the duke, arrive. Expressing a widely held view of the rogues' role, Robert Shulman states: "The Duke and the Dauphin are a parody of the positive family Huck and Jim create. . . . [S]ince [their] acquisitive motives and values are central to American society, the Duke and the Dauphin also comically image the society they fleece."[11] The analysis of the impostor's behavior as a mirror of the society is precise; if, however, Huck's relations with Jim fit this description, the rogues would not have been on the raft in the first place.

The king and the duke are frequently portrayed, whether explicitly or implicitly, as invaders. The reality is quite different: it is Huck who rescues them from the townspeople pursuing them, and then brings them aboard the raft. Having had Pap as a model, he should have known that raffish outsiders can be as dangerous as respectable insiders; but his identification with marginal white males eclipses any thought of the danger they present to Jim. As a result, the boy who rescued Jim from one pair of slavecatchers delivers him to another.

With the entrance of the rogues, fantasized identities mushroom: the pair metamorphose into the rightful King of France and the Duke of Bridgewater, not to mention such other personalities as (drunken) temperance lecturer and Shakespearean actors. The two pretenders would have envied those debt-ridden slaveowners who fled to other states and, whatever else they left behind, retained a standing determined by the human property they kept. Aside from that conferred by their skin, the king and the duke have no status they can publicly reveal. But their proclamations on the raft of royal birth, which would mark them as lunatics onshore, allow them to assume instant dominion over Huck and Jim, who are initially delighted to be in the company of royalty.[12]

For Huck, thrilled by the rascals' rehearsals for their pseudo-Shakespearean performances, the raft is a "most uncommon lively place" (chap. 21). But soon the raft that traveled only by night to shield Jim from slavehunters travels night and/or day, the better to put distance between the impostors and the townspeople they defraud. Ostensibly to protect him, but actually to protect him from other bounty-seekers, the duke prints a handbill offering a reward for a runaway Louisiana slave whose description fits Jim to perfection. If anyone comes near the raft, declares the duke, they will tie Jim up and say they are going South to get the reward. Jim soon spends his time tied up, while Huck accompanies the rascals on their shoreside scams.

Although it is not easy to believe that Huck would have been gullible enough to accept the pair as royalty, he does, at least, quickly realize they are frauds. As for Jim, that he is a fugitive slave should make him more not less acute than a white adult (a point acknowledged upon occasion even by members of the slaveholding class),[13] let alone a white child. Even when the ragged, dirty, smelly rogues openly admit they are fake royalty ("It ain't my fault I warn't born a duke, it ain't your fault you warn't born a king" [chap. 19]), Jim gives no sign of catching on. His aberrant lack of awareness that the pair are dangerous frauds causes him suffering not only from the impostors but also from Huck, who decides not to share his own awareness with Jim.

Whether Jim ever realizes that the rogues are not royalty remains ambiguous, but he cannot avoid recognizing that they menace him. Without overtly acknowledging his fears, he pleads, comically and piteously, with Huck to break with them. Huck resists. When Jim complains that they are "rapscallions," Huck insists that, as royalty, they cannot help being rapscallions. Often praised for his "moral lies," Huck also reveals his handiness with the other kind when he tells the reader a different story: "What was the use to tell Jim these warn't real kings and dukes? It wouldn't a done no good" (chap. 23). Obviously, Huck's concern is not that Jim wouldn't believe him, but that Jim would.

Huck's reasons for not wanting to break with the rascals are obscure. The excitement they brought with them has palled. And if he fears they know too much about him, or the physical harm they could inflict, it seems he would enlist Jim as an ally and exhibit his flair for escape. Perhaps Huck resists a break because of his lingering identification with the pair, whom he calls "family," "our tribe," "our gang" (chaps. 19, 27). Even when he expresses disgust with their hypocrisy, he grants them a status he denies to blacks: "Well, if ever I struck anything like it, I'm a nigger. It was enough to make a body ashamed of the human race" (chap. 24).

III

Jim's reaction when Huck refuses to break with the frauds seems mild. Peculiarly mild. So mild that one may suspect that mildness is a mask for his real feelings. That Jim's temperate reactions often veil his emotions may be inferred from the glints of aggression and resentment that occasionally pierce his pliant demeanor. The first such suggestion, which is made in so farcical a way that a reader is apt not to take it seriously, comes in the scene where Jim expresses disbelief that men speak French. Huck asks:

> "Spose a man was to come to you and say *Polly-vous-franzy*—what would you think?"
> "I wouldn' think nuff'n; I'd take en bust him over de head. Dat is, ef he warn't white. I wouldn't 'low no nigger to call me dat." (Chap. 14)

Jim's anxiety to assure Huck he would never dream of hitting a white man who offends him suggests that is exactly what he would do if he could. Jim knows, of course, that a black who hits a white, no matter the reason, may well face death.[14]

The second instance hinting that Jim has hidden feelings occurs just after he hears of the duke's threatening plan to travel by day as well as night. The rogues are asleep in the sheltered places on the raft they have usurped from Huck and Jim, while Huck and Jim are unprotected from a thunderstorm. When Huck is washed overboard, Jim forgoes his customary concern for "honey" and laughs uproariously. "It most killed Jim a-laughing," says Huck, who adds: "He was the easiest nigger to laugh that ever was, anyway" (chap. 20). If Jim is so quick to laugh, it seems odd that Huck waits until he is halfway through his book to mention it. By choosing this moment to convert Jim into a laughing "darky," Huck can dismiss even a fleeting notion that Jim may have good reason to enjoy a laugh—without a touch of servility or protestations of affection—at his expense.

That Jim's passivity may veil contrary traits is also displayed in quite a different way. At night Huck sometimes hears him "moaning and mourning" for his wife and children, and with a notable, if transient, tact and sympathy, pretends not to hear. Although he finds it disturbing to the "natural" order, Huck concludes that Jim cares for his family just as much as whites do for theirs (Pap's son has no doubt the reader will accept him as an authority on parental devotion).[15] One night Jim speaks of his anguish over the way he treated his four-year-old daughter, who had recently recovered from scarlet fever. He tells her to shut the door. After she seems to disobey his order a third time, he shouts, "I lay I *make* you mine!" and sends her sprawling with a slap to the head. The child cries. Jim is about to hit her again when the wind slams the door shut and she does not move. He pleads with God to forgive him because he will never forgive himself: "O, she was plumb deef en dumb, Huck, plumb deef en dumb—en I'd ben a treat'n her so!" (chap. 23).

So glaring is the contrast between Huck's racist attitude toward blacks as parents and Jim's love for his children that one's attention is apt to be diverted from the fact that, even in retrospect, Jim is rueful only because the child he hit could not hear.[16] That he still believes his treatment of his child would otherwise have been proper suggests he acted in accord with accepted standards in slave communities. There surely were slaves who took out their desperation on their children, but this was not the usual impetus for discipline. If Jim had been attempting to instill obedience in his daughter because an enslaved child had to learn to listen to her parents for her own protection, he would have acted in keeping with the mores of the slaves—whose basic purpose in disciplining was to teach their children that they must protect themselves and other blacks from the dangers presented by whites.[17]

These hints that Jim conceals resentment and hostility suggest why the masters feared their slaves and, perhaps in part to cope with their dread, divided them into two categories, "good nigger" and "bad nigger." That the owners' judgment was, even on their own terms, none too astute is illustrated by the many slaves who were classified "good niggers" until they ran away. Because the fugitive slave was an iconic "bad nigger," Jim's aggression is particularly threatening; even though it is directed against his own child, it could be rechanneled.

So the passage in which Jim reveals aggression is followed by one signaling that his aggression has been brought under control. After he says how hard it is to lie roped all day while the others are ashore, the duke pretends to meet his complaint. Making sure Jim will be bound to the raft until he can be sold, the duke dresses him in a long gown from a King Lear costume, adds white hair and whiskers, paints him a "dead dull solid blue," and puts up a sign, "*Sick Arab— but harmless when not out of his head.*" He also tells Jim that if anyone draws near the raft, he must "carry on a little, and fetch a howl or two like a wild beast" (chap. 24). Eric Lott reveals the ancestry of this passage by pointing to a connection between what he calls "Arabface" and blackface. Lott also contends, however, that at the same time Jim's appearance "recalls the art of blackface," it "explodes the very idea of racial performance."[18] One might well argue that the passage exploits rather than explodes the idea of racial performance. Nor should the implications of the costume Jim is put into be overlooked.

Where fugitive slaves changed their own identities, Jim's changes of identities are imposed on him by whites. In this case, his grotesque feminization via the gown signals that he has "womanly" traits such as passivity and helplessness, which the slaveowners ascribed to blacks of both genders. On the other hand, an animalistic touch of maleness (horsehair whiskers) signals that the brutal and licentious traits the slaveowners attributed to blacks—that is, the traits they transferred to blacks from their own behavior toward blacks—have been neutered in Jim. Thus Jim's costume personifies the slaveowners' "good nigger"/"bad nigger" dichotomy: he is "harmless" (that is, docile) unless "out of his head" (that is, rebellious). As Mary Kemp Davis notes, Jim's dress is a "visual emblem of his symbolic castration," which "signifies that the community has subdued the 'bad nigger' whose goals are antithetical to the community's."[19]

7 | Conscience Revisited

I

"If idealized research could have looked into the hearts of its Southern white subjects in those years, it would have found them bleeding hardly one drop for the oppressed blacks. Instead, they would have seen hearts stoutly thumping with assurance that they beat in rhythm with heavenly drums."[1] This seems to be a deadly accurate description of the real-life counterparts of the white characters in *Huckleberry Finn,* right down to the religious sanctification of their behavior. In fact, it is a description by the Southern historian Joel Williamson of the Southern whites who lived a century after the time in which the novel is set, and who were the subjects of Gunnar Myrdal's *An American Dilemma.*

According to Myrdal, whites were in inner conflict over their belief in a creed of equality and opportunity on the one hand, and their treatment of blacks on the other.[2] It is singular that *An American Dilemma,* the most influential study dealing with black and white in America, and *Huckleberry Finn,* the most influential novel dealing with black and white in America, are at odds on this matter: while Myrdal visualized whites whose consciences bother them because of their treatment of blacks, Twain visualized a white whose conscience tells him it is sinful to rescue a black from slavery.

Certainly *Huck Finn*'s reputation as a historically authentic work may be traced in large part to Twain's penetratingly ironic handling of the consciences of whites in slaveholding states, who believed, or were led to believe, that abolitionism was the sin. Still, the history of white Americans cannot be divorced from that of African Americans. Thus, if *Huck Finn* sends a fugitive slave South, one must also expect a certain nonchalance in its treatment of whites—as, for example, when the dying Miss Watson's conscience impels her to reward her runaway slave by freeing him. Although the treatment of other whites is generally more plausible, it too weaves in and out of authenticity. Take, for instance, three white characters through whom Twain makes complex social comments: Pap, Judith Loftus, and Colonel Sherburn.

II

When Charles Miner Thompson spoke of Huck Finn's "strong and struggling moral nature, so notably Anglo-Saxon," he engaged in selective amnesia. As one who embraced claims of Anglo-Saxon moral superiority, he would necessarily have embraced those of Irish moral inferiority. In permitting Huck's skin color to annul the connotations of his surname, Thompson also overlooked that during the period in which *Huck Finn* is set (and beyond), the Irish were not accepted as "white": "Nativist folk wisdom held that an Irishman was a 'nigger,' inside out"; or, as a pseudoscientific notion put it, that the "Irish were part of a separate caste or a 'dark' race, possibly originally African," points out David Roediger.[3]

Since the Irish were oppressed in their own country, and because Ireland had antislavery traditions, the new arrivals were receptive to abolitionism. But under the aegis of anti-abolitionist Northerners, a complex process was initiated. Via the rewards associated with being "white," as well as the penalties associated with being "black," Irish immigrants were converted from a group whose sympathies seemed naturally to lie with the antislavery cause to a group with members who became both leaders and participants in bloody antiblack riots in such cities as New York and Philadelphia.[4]

That the Irish were not regarded as "white" also casts an ironic light on Huck's description of Pap's skin as "not like another man's white, but a white to make a body sick, a white to make a body's flesh crawl—a tree-toad white, a fish-belly white." Even though *Huck Finn's* nineteenth-century readers were likely to be influenced by anti-Irish attitudes, these words carried essentially the same message they send today: that Pap is different from other whites (at least if they are not poor ones)—different not only in his failure to conform to social standards, but also in his racial attitudes.[5] But Pap's opinions are not anomalous, or even restricted to poor whites; his noted diatribe on blacks and the vote, which appears to set him apart from respectable whites, actually does the opposite.

Pap, who says he would have gone to the polls if he hadn't been too drunk to get there, swears never to vote again after hearing that a "mulatter" from Ohio, who is "most as white as a white man," could "*vote*, when he was at home." The man, says Pap, wears the "whitest" shirt, the "shiniest" hat, and has a gold watch and a silver-headed cane. He is a "p'fessor in a college" who can "talk all kinds of languages," who "knowed everything." When the professor fails to step aside for Pap ("And to see the cool way of that nigger"), Pap shoves him off the road. Demanding to know why he hasn't been put on the auction block, Pap is informed by bystanders ("the people") that a free black must be in the state six months before he can be sold. "Here's a govment that calls itself a govment . . . and yet's got to set stock-still for six whole months before it can take ahold of a prowling, thieving, infernal white-shirted free nigger" (chap. 6).

The supposedly great divide between Pap and respectable citizens narrows if a reader detaches Pap's sentiments from his disreputable character. Not only would proper, well-to-do townspeople be as outraged as Pap at a black man's voting; they would also be as furious as the ragged Pap at the sight of a well-dressed free black, albeit for a different reason: they would regard him as a deplorable example for their slaves. And however critical the respectable ones might otherwise be of Pap, none would reprimand him for pushing a black man off the road; on the contrary, a good many would have scoffed at his singular restraint.

That Pap's sentiments were rife among whites rather than peculiar to poor ones is illustrated by the fact that it is difficult to separate

Twain's fictional Missouri, which allows free blacks to be put on the auction block in six months, from the real Missouri of 1835. In that year, which corresponds with the first year of *Huck Finn*'s time frame (the novel is set somewhere between 1835 and 1844), the state legislature ordered that free blacks between the ages of seven and twenty-one be bound out as apprentices or servants; the state, in other words, "enslave[d] them by another name." And that same year, the legislature also decreed that to live in the state, free blacks had to be licensed; the license, which required them to post bond or have whites put up security, would be in effect only so long as the licensee exhibited "good behavior."[6] Clearly, the state could make such demands only because it implicitly classified blacks in the same way Pap did, as criminals. (As for the free black man voting in Ohio, he could not have done so there either.)

The incident also serves as an allegory for the era in which Twain wrote his novel, when African Americans were being disfranchised by violent means. These implications are, however, ambiguous. It is ironic that the most learned black male cannot vote in Missouri while a Pap can. At the same time, though, the incident implies that the franchise should be linked to formal education and, more subtly, to property.[7] During Reconstruction, when the ex-slaveowners were by far the most educated group and the ex-slaves the least, African Americans cast their ballots for and held office in governments that enacted remarkable democratic and social measures, while their ex-masters engaged in a campaign that drove the South backwards.

It is plausible that the novel's free black man would be light-skinned, since mulattoes were freed at a vastly disproportionate rate.[8] But irrespective of the author's intentions, the treatment of this almost-white character evokes notions of racially determined traits. In the nineteenth century, hereditarians claimed that blood is the carrier of racially superior or inferior traits (the role twentieth-century hereditarians assign to genes). Thus the professor's "white blood" would no doubt have been taken by many, if not most, earlier readers as the explanation for both his prodigious accomplishments and his daring resistance to racist aggression: "Mulattoes . . . were often described as rebellious and intelligent," notes James Oliver Horton.[9] The presence of this character also invites comparison with Jim: the light-skinned African American is a master of languages, while the dark-skinned one believes all men speak the same language; the almost-white professor is rebellious, while the dark-skinned fugitive is compliant.

Pap is set apart not only by skin that is "not like another man's white," but also by a seemingly inverse means: he delivers his monologue in blackface. "A body would a thought he was Adam, he was just all mud," Huck says of Pap (chap. 6), who has spent the night in a gutter.[10] Might any subversive connotations be attached to this scene? Since Huck identifies Pap with Adam, who was created from wet earth, might this be taken as a metaphor for the common origins of blacks and whites? Not likely. Or might the fact that the "fish-belly white" Pap is black and the black professor white encourage a reader to see black and white as mutable constructs rather than biological categories? Hardly, considering that the identification of black with baseness and white (except for the fish-belly variety) with elevation conforms to preconceptions.

The scene also has an affinity with minstrelsy in that its dominant antiblack sentiments are accompanied by anti-elitist ones—that is, Pap's diatribe includes a comic castigation of the government for denying him his "rights" to his son's money (chap. 6). The treatment of the light-skinned African American is also influenced by minstrelsy. While Pap may embellish the professor's outfit (the "whitest shirt," the "shiniest hat"), an ensemble featuring silver and gold accessories hardly elicits the image of a professor on a visit to a village, let alone a black one who wishes to survive his trip down to what may have been his home state. Instead it summons up the "dandy," a stock figure that merged minstrelsy's ridicule of the elite with its primary theme, ridicule of blacks.

III

Pap has achieved legendary status as a figure presumably emblematic of poor whites. But the category "poor white" encompassed diverse nonlandholding whites in the slave states, and *Huck Finn* mirrors this. Where, for instance, the novel presents a parasitical, self-loathing poor white in Pap, it presents a hard-working, self-respecting one in Judith Loftus, the woman Huck encounters when he returns to town dressed as a girl. However, at the same time that the novel shows Loftus as a smart and capable woman, it also reveals—with a compelling authenticity—contamination at the source of her self-esteem.

Mrs. Loftus tells a tale that suggests how hard it was for poor whites in search of a living.[11] She also tells Huck that some think "old Finn" killed his son, while others think it was done by the "runaway nigger." After unmasking Huck as a female impersonator, she quickly reassures him: "I ain't going to hurt you, and I ain't going to tell on you, nuther. You just tell me your secret, and trust me. I'll keep it; and what's more, I'll help you. So'll my old man, if you want him to. You see, you're a runaway 'prentice—that's all. It ain't anything. There ain't any harm in it. You've been treated bad, and you made up your mind to cut. Bless you, child, I wouldn't tell on you" (chap. 11). While many slaveholding women offer Huck maternal kindness, the nonslaveholding Judith Loftus also offers him solidarity. But Mrs. Loftus, who would never tell on a runaway apprentice, is eager to tell on a runaway slave. Mr. Loftus, whose solidarity his wife so confidently proffers to the supposed apprentice, is out hunting for Jim. "Does three hundred dollars lay round every day for people to pick up?" exclaims Mrs. Loftus in anticipation of the reward (chap. 11).

Mr. Loftus would no doubt have been prepared for slavehunting by serving in a slave patrol, service that, typically, was obligatory (sometimes without pay) for white males of military age. "The patrol had authority not only over slaves, but over free blacks as well, and over any white person who might be suspected of conspiring with blacks in illegal activities. It was, in short, a system in which virtually all white men came together to enforce the racial establishment. In the patrol every white man was a policeman in the face of every black person," states Williamson.[12]

IV

Where Judith Loftus is a poor white whose conscience is split along the color line, Colonel Sherburn—an aristocrat of Bricksville, that most depraved of towns—is, like Pap, minus a conscience. Fascinating as drama, the Bricksville sequence is not organic to the novel. With Huck serving as a device that plays back Sherburn's voice, the episode appears to exist primarily as social comment. But exactly what comment does it make?

A recurring interpretation sees the episode as a condemnation of lynching expressed through Sherburn; an oft-cited basis for this view is an expurgated passage from *Life on the Mississippi* (1883) in which Twain expresses opinions similar to certain of Sherburn's. A number of critics also see the episode as an allegory for the time when Twain wrote *Huck Finn*. The sequence has two distinct parts. In the first, Sherburn cold-bloodedly murders Boggs, a comically harmless, drunken, poor farmer who has accused him of swindling (a charge not dispelled); in the second, according to various critics, he redeems himself by standing off a lynch mob.

For instance, in an apparent effort to reconcile Sherburn as cold-blooded murderer with Sherburn as courageous opponent of a mob, David E. E. Sloane speaks of "the aristocratic code of honor as practiced by Colonel Sherburn" and the "degraded code of unregulated lynch law as seen in the Bricksville loafers." Sloane also states that Sherburn offers a "full analysis of lynch law."[13] The point that Sherburn is a surrogate for Twain was first made explicit by Philip S. Foner: "Twain's hatred of and contempt for lynchers was brilliantly expressed in the powerful scene . . . where Colonel [Sherburn's] scorn withers the bravados of the mob."[14] If Sherburn speaks for Twain (whose post–Civil War antilynching views Foner cites), his remarks also have allegorical implications for the period when Twain wrote *Huck Finn*. Walter Blair states: "When [Twain] wrote this attack on lynching . . . he was hitting at a contemporary evil. . . . The mob on a murderous rampage was a very present danger when Twain wrote about the march on Sherburn's house."[15] Michael Egan concurs: "Twain avoids an overt reference to the Ku-Klux Klan . . . but his meaning is clear."[16] But is it?

The intended lynching of Sherburn begins when the white male witnesses to the murder, portrayed as sadistic and voyeuristic, coalesce into a mob and race through town, snatching up clotheslines along the way. Blacks race out of the mob's reach; black women cry.[17]

Surely, it seems, an allegory is developing for the time when Ku Klux Klan lynchings were on the rise. But the hint of an analogy is fleeting. For one thing, unlike KKK/white supremacist lynchings, the attempted lynching in Bricksville bears the marks of "frontier justice," which once usurped legally sanctioned trials in certain areas of the country.

That summary justice would erupt in Bricksville is hardly surprising, given that a murder in broad daylight in the center of town elicits no sign of the law. The Bricksville incident also has another defining feature: the resentment of lower-class whites against upper-class justice. There are courts, we learn, but they will surely not convict a local aristocrat for murdering a nobody.[18] Thus where the Bricksville mob sets out to avenge a crime its members have witnessed and for which they know the perpetrator will not be punished, the white supremacist mob's classic modus operandi was to fabricate criminal charges and then lynch those it accused.[19]

When the men reach Sherburn's house, he is standing on his porch roof with a double-barreled shotgun in his hands. Although one would expect the Bricksville ruffians also to carry guns, this is a staged drama in which the dramatist tells us only that they have clotheslines. While Twain's stationing of Sherburn above the mob undoubtedly has metaphorical implications, it also has practical ones: the only man we know to be armed is strategically placed to dispatch anyone who threatens him.

Addressing the mob, Sherburn exclaims: "The idea of *you* lynching anybody! . . . Because you're brave enough to tar and feather poor friendless cast-out women, . . . did that make you think you had grit enough to lay your hands on a *man!*" (chap. 22). Thus Sherburn maintains that his "manliness" is his shield, when in fact he is protected by his status as a local aristocrat, not to mention his gun. By contrast, the members of the mob, who are quite safe if they go after a sanctioned victim, endanger themselves if they carry out their threat against Sherburn.

As Sherburn continues, it becomes increasingly evident that he is not denouncing lynching but the cowardice of the "average man." He castigates juries for acquitting murderers for fear of being shot in the back by a murderer's friends. After an acquittal, "a *man* goes in the night, with a hundred masked cowards at his back, and lynches the rascal" (chap. 22). If it seems paradoxical that a *man* would require a hundred cowards at his back or, rather, that a *man* would lead a lynch mob, Sherburn sees no incongruity; on the contrary, since he regards lynching as a corrective to judicial cowardice, the lynchers must be led by a fearless figure. (Given that Sherburn is scornful rather than ironic, it is not surprising that he fails to notice the irony of his complaint that juries acquit murderers.)

Although the Bricksville incident reflects the traditional assumption that mobs were formed by lower-class whites, it also portrays an upper-class white as an exponent of lynching. In fact, elite whites led and/or sanctioned mob violence in the antebellum South, during Reconstruction (ex-Confederate officers, in particular), and long after.[20] If Sherburn's speech is recognized as a sanction, not a condemnation, of lynching, it is possible (albeit with some difficulty) to see in it allegorical implications for Reconstruction and later eras.

To say that Colonel Sherburn's speech has these implications is certainly not to say that this was Twain's intent. His intentions are opaque. The critical opinion that Sherburn speaks for Twain recognizes the likenesses in their views (both denounce the cowardice of the average man, both admire the bold lone bandit)[21] but does not recognize that Sherburn endorses the practice Twain condemns.

Twain's suppression of the passage on lynching in *Life on the Mississippi* suggests that the man who wrote so indelibly of Huck's battles with his conscience was no stranger to bouts with his own, which apparently continued late into his life. "I shouldn't have even half a friend left down there, after it issued from the press," he said as he decided, shortly after the turn of the century, to drop a contemplated history of lynching.[22] He also decided against publishing an essay on lynching that he had already written. His fear of offending Southern readers—a fear that accounted not only for his suppression of two statements on lynching but may also have affected what he wrote in them[23]—might explain the convolutions and opacity of the Bricksville sequence.

This fear may also suggest why he did not carry out a plan he envisioned in his notes for the novel: "They lynch a free nigger."[24] The note seems to refer to the latter part of the book, and possibly to Jim. Jim's captors, who do not know he has been freed, want to lynch the runaway as an example to other blacks, and also because he is suspected of plotting an insurrection (Tom Sawyer's dangerous games create the misapprehension). The would-be lynchers are stopped by cooler heads who warn that "his owner would turn up and make us pay for him, sure" (chap. 42). If Twain had decided to have Jim lynched, he could simply have let the hotheads prevail (as they no doubt would have in the case of a fugitive slave suspected of insurrection). Nonetheless, Twain makes a telling point in showing that Jim's only protection is, as Quirk observes, "the mistaken belief that he is a slave and therefore a white man's property."[25]

This peculiar protection, though, does not apply to the free black who defies Pap's order to move aside and, despite the presence of "the people," miraculously emerges with no more than a shove. If, however, Twain had allowed the free black to be so much as threatened with lynching on election day, he would have confronted his readers with the most volatile of allegories for the time in which *Huck Finn* was published.

8 | Family Values

I

Huckleberry Finn is "a hymn to an older America forever gone, an America which had its great national faults, which was full of violence and even of cruelty, but which still maintained its sense of reality, for it was not yet enthralled by money," declared Trilling.[1] If *Huck Finn* is a hymn, it celebrates some strange things; indeed, it would be difficult to find a novel where the characters are more enthralled by money, driven by the search for it, ready to commit violence on its behalf, or more victimized by others' lust for it. This hardly seems surprising, given that the society trades in human beings.

A compelling instance of the consequences of money-lust in a slaveholding society occurs in the Wilks episode, the sequence in which Huck is confronted with the second of his three moral crises. There is a significant difference between Huck's crisis in this instance and his other two. During his first, when his conscience besieges him because he does not tell the slavehunters the truth, and during his ultimate one, when he decides to go to hell rather than allow Jim to remain a slave, the distance between the authorial voice and the narrator's is as palpable as the distance between two poles. To search for the author's voice at crucial points in the Wilks sequence, though, is to feel as if one is in a canyon, hearing many voices but unable to discern the one that set them off.

According to the prevailing interpretation of this episode, Huck, inspired in particular by Mary Jane Wilks, successfully passes his moral test, which helps prepare him for his ultimate crisis of conscience over Jim.[2] This interpretation, which takes Huck at his word, overlooks his ability to play the trickster, even when he may not be fully conscious of doing so. As he tells it, the only moral decision he faces involves the Wilks sisters. But his moral crisis is created by a fraud in which he is implicated, and its repercussions are infinitely greater for another family, the black one the Wilkses own, than it is for the Wilkses. The question then is, how does Huck's resolution of the crisis affect the black family?

II

In the Wilks episode, the king and the duke, having learned of the money left by the late Peter Wilks, pose as his brothers, one a minister, the other deaf and mute. With Huck cast as their servant, they have supposedly come from England to see Peter before he dies. Huck's scathing commentary on their venality and hypocrisy, as well as that of the villagers, lends his voice a particular authority. This in turn encourages the reader to believe what he says about himself and also about Mary Jane, with whom he is smitten.

After the three sisters rapturously welcome them, the king enhances his and the duke's identities as Peter Wilks's brothers by brandishing sundry names and facts gleaned along the way, and by turning over to the sisters the six thousand dollars Peter left his brothers (the rascals plan to steal it back). An old family friend denounces the king as a fraud, telling Mary Jane that she accepts "empty names and facts" as "*proofs*," and begs her to turn the rascal out. "*Here* is my answer," she retorts, as she gives the gold back to the king. The assembled mourners clap and stomp with approval. "Mary Jane straightened herself up, and my, but she was handsome!" exclaims Huck (chap. 25). Thus Huck overlooks that Mary Jane has openly scorned an old friend to the delight of the mourners/mob, who "looked hungry" at the sight of the gold (chap. 25). At the same time, she has also acted in a way that surely finds a response in Huck's heart: in her joyous belief that she has been united with her uncles, she has shown, however foolishly, that money is not her only concern.

At a supper for the mourners, Huck serves the rogues, while the slaves wait on the other diners. He is then relegated to the kitchen to eat leftovers with the youngest sister, Joanna, who has a harelip. Joanna is curious about life in England, particularly as to whether the English treat their servants "better'n we treat our niggers." In an odd rejoinder from one who excludes blacks from the human race, Huck assures her, "A servant ain't nobody, there" (chap. 26). Although she sees nothing peculiar in an English boy's defaming his own country in favor of the late colony, Joanna is otherwise quite a clever girl (this, however, does not work to her advantage, since her brightness is converted into a liability by its traditionalist connection with physical unattractiveness).

Mary Jane overhears Joanna informing Huck that she has caught him in a maze of lies about England. Having exiled Joanna to the kitchen so the mourners' supper will not be spoiled by the sight of a harelip, Mary Jane mercilessly berates her sister for being unkind to a stranger. When Joanna attempts to tell her what Huck said, Mary Jane insists: "It don't make no difference what he *said*. . . . The thing is for you to treat him *kind*, and not be saying things to make him remember he ain't in his own country and amongst his own folks" (chap. 26). Although Mary Jane's unconscious parody of the rules of hospitality thwarts the unmasking of a fraud, her words resonate for the boy who has no folks of his own. Huck is appalled at himself, remorseful for having let the rogues rob the sisters. He resolves to get the sisters' money back for them.

Huck is virtually led to the money by the two thieves, who are foiled by their racist assumptions: "do you reckon a nigger can run across money and not borrow some of it?" the duke rhetorically demands of the king (chap. 26). The pair stuff the gold into a mattress, where it will be safe because a "nigger" turns one over only about twice a year. Huck, listening surreptitiously, soon takes the gold and hides it in Peter Wilks's coffin. When the rascals discover the money is missing, they cross-examine Huck, who need say no more than that he saw the slaves go into the king's room.

Huck is "dreadful glad" that he "worked it all off onto the niggers and yet hadn't done the niggers no harm by it" (chap. 27). Huck's apparent elation, not to mention his self-congratulation for having done a good deed, is curious, since blaming the blacks does them no harm only because they have already been sold by the king, the mother separately from her sons, and taken off by slavetraders. Huck's self-praise is all the more peculiar because of his own implication in the rascals' scheme. Nonetheless, the only moral responsibility he acknowledges is to the white family.

Before the funeral, the king announced that he had to settle the estate and return to his congregation; he would, he said, take the girls with him. The sisters, euphoric at the prospect of England, tell him to "sell out as quick" as he wants. When the king puts everything up for sale, Huck is heartsick at the deception of the sisters, but sees no "safe way" to speak up. The first sale is made when two slavetraders buy the slaves ("away they went," says Huck). The sisters express shock: "The girls said they hadn't ever dreamed of seeing the family separated or sold away from the town" (chap. 27).

Never dreamed of it? These daughters of a master (their father also owned a tannery and several houses) have surely known since early childhood that slave families are separated and sold off. Yet in their bliss about going to England, the sisters urge a quick sale of their property. There is quite a stir among townspeople who disapprove of the family's separation; although they put the blame on the "uncles," they would know—as Mary Jane is certainly aware—that mother and sons could not have been separated had she not unconditionally consented to the disposal of her property.[3]

Huck's remarks about the black family are also singular. In other episodes, he veers between referring to blacks by their names and as "niggers," but he speaks of the Wilks slaves only as "the niggers." Nor does he report a word they say. By granting them no semblance of individual identity, but instead confining them to a dehumanizing category, he suggests an unconscious desire to distance himself, as well as the reader, from them. His description of their departure also hints at this subliminal wish: "I thought them poor girls and them niggers would break their hearts for grief." So, while Huck cannot deny the slaves' grief, his sympathy is confined to the sisters. But this apparent effort to keep the blacks beyond the pale of compassion is not totally successful, since his elision in an ensuing sentence of a second "them" suggests ambivalence: "I can't ever get it out of my memory, the sight of them poor miserable girls and niggers hanging around each other's necks and crying" (chap. 27).

Huck's portrait of the departure is also ambiguous in other ways. Why do the slaves embrace the sisters? Are they brokenhearted at parting from beloved young mistresses? Huck's praise of Mary Jane encourages us to think so, and she is certainly no icily distant mistress. Still, one may wonder how the imperious, mercurial temperament she displays with whites manifests itself each day with blacks. In any event, would the slaves not be bitter at her and her sisters for their heedless consent to the sale of their property? Might they not be making a last plea for the sisters to do something, anything, to keep mother and sons together? And what of Mary Jane's tears? Surely she is sorrowful about the slaves, but is her sorrow not compounded by guilt for her unthinking consent to the sale, as well as shame at what the villagers may think of her?

As he watches the parting, Huck says he would have had to "bust out and tell on our gang" had he not known the sale was fraudulent and the slaves would soon be back (chap. 27). He does not explain why a fraudulent sale of slaves is self-correcting. After the black family is gone, Huck finds Mary Jane alone and crying ("to think they ain't *ever* going to see each other any more!"). Now Huck exclaims: "I'll tell you how I know the niggers will see each other again—inside of two weeks—here in this house—and *prove* how I know it" (chap. 28). Huck then proves, or rather attests, that her supposed uncles are impostors. Revealing the uncles are fakes, though, is hardly proof that he knows why the slaves will be back (let alone in two weeks); on the contrary, that a fraudulent sale can proceed with such ease suggests it will be virtually impossible to undo. But if the slaves will soon be back, as Huck promises, there is no need to take action to bring them back, which would entail informing friends of the Wilkses' of his own part in the hoax.

Having guaranteed Mary Jane that her slaves will reappear shortly, Huck can turn his attention to another matter: making sure she will stay mum until he can get away. If she lets on about the frauds before then, Huck tells her, the town will rescue him from their claws but someone else will be in "big trouble" (chap. 28). While Huck is surely concerned for Jim, he cannot really believe the villagers would make trouble only for Jim; after all, if Jim is discovered, Huck's secret will also come out—making it likely that he too would have to be res-cued from the villagers (who soon call for drowning the rogues, rid-ing them out of town on a rail, lynching them—and also their co-hort Huck). And perhaps he might also have to be rescued from Mary Jane ("we'll have them tarred and feathered, and flung in the river!" she proclaims when Huck tells her that her "uncles" are frauds [chap. 28]).

Even as Huck assures Mary Jane that her slaves will be back within two weeks, the family members are being thrust ever further into ir-retrievability. The slavetraders undoubtedly supplied fake identities, since they did not pay in cash but gave the gullible king "three-day drafts" (chap. 27). One trader took the mother to New Orleans, the other took the sons to Memphis—or so they said. The traders would have sold the family members, either in the slave markets in those cities or elsewhere, to two or even three buyers, who may have kept them or resold them; the unknown owners, whose identities may also be open to question, could then have taken the grieving family mem-bers anywhere.[4] Another unknowable is the mother and sons; slaves sold away from family and friends sometimes resisted their fate through suicide.[5]

Although Huck has seen so much of deception, disappearance, and death that even his fantasies teem with white family members who die or go off never to return, he guarantees that the black family members will soon be back. If he were convinced, though, of what he promises, why can he never get the sight of "them poor miserable girls and niggers" out of his memory? Why, in retrospect, is that scene of separation not replaced by a vision of reunion? As for Mary Jane, just as she instantly accepted the rascals' empty proof of identity, she instantly accepts Huck's empty proof of reunion.

At the same time, whatever concern he has for himself, Huck's concern for Jim is genuine. This raises a question: if he had spoken up to stop the sale of the Wilks slaves, would he not have put Jim as well as himself at greater risk? Quite aside from the fact that he does not hesitate to put Jim at risk to help the Wilks sisters, let alone by his connection with the rascals, the matter is irrelevant: because he never acknowledges a moral obligation to the black family, the question of morality and conflicting obligations never arises.

Although the time Huck buys for his getaway by promising the slaves' prompt return also provides the slavetraders with more time to transport them beyond the realm of reclaim, there is no reason to think he is conscious of what he does. He is so inundated with lies, those he hears and those he tells, that he may have difficulty, particularly when in a close place, in distinguishing falsity from truth. If Huck is unaware of his untruth, surely Twain was not.[6] Still, he encourages his readers to believe Huck's porous promise of the slaves' return. Had he done otherwise, he would have cast a narrator who is implicated in the hoax that leads to the black family's sale in a distressfully harsh light.

Were it not for the happy ending Huck affixes to a tragedy, the slaves' departure would be the emotional peak of the episode. Instead that function is taken over by his parting from Mary Jane. Before he takes his leave, she says she will pray for him. "Pray for me! . . . But I bet she done it. . . . She had the grit to pray for Judas" (chap. 28). One may wonder why Huck identifies himself with Judas. Is it only because he has betrayed the sanctified institution of slavery by consorting with a fugitive slave? Or is it also because he knows that however long Mary Jane waits, her slaves will not return?

III

When Huck guarantees that the slaves will soon be back, the novel undergoes a seismic shift: instead of demonstrating that cruelty and deceit lie at the heart of the society, it tells us that the society undoes fraud and mends heartbreak. Or, to be exact, the narrator tells us this, while the author, by providing his narrator with empty promises of a happy ending, distantly hints at a different story, that is, the one he has been telling all along. The novel returns overtly to the latter mode after Huck, who failed to anticipate that the rascals might also escape, discovers they have sold Jim. Huck sits down and cries. But, he tells us, not for long.

Moving consciously, deliberately into his trickster mode, Huck asks a local boy if he knows anything about a "runaway nigger." The boy tells where Jim is being held, and asks if Huck is looking for him. Huck replies:

> "You bet I ain't! I run across him in the woods . . . and he said if I hollered he'd cut my livers out—and told me to lay down and stay where I was. . . . Been there ever since; afeard to come out."
> "Well," he says, "you needn't be afeard no more, becuz they've got him. . . . "
> "It's a good job they got him."
> "Well, I *reckon!* There's two hunderd dollars reward on him. It's like picking up money out'n the road."
> "Yes, it is—and *I* could a had it if I'd been big enough." (Chap. 31)

Huck has demonstrated yet another way of masking identity: instead of offering a false vita, he presents a defining worldview, one proclaiming that he, a stranger, is trustworthy because his beliefs are exactly the ones he would have if he lived there. Like his fake identities, the views he presents are not entirely alien to Huck. To be sure, when he laments that he has missed out on the reward, there is not the slightest doubt he is dissembling for the boy's benefit; the model offered by Miss Watson, Judith Loftus, the slavehunters, and society in general—the one the local boy has so thirstily absorbed—never tempts Huck. On the other hand, when he asserts that the runaway threatened to "cut my livers out," Huck echoes the masters' tales. Under other circumstances, he would quite likely be susceptible to these same stories, which denied the justice of a slave's use of violent means to prevent capture, while ignoring the slaveowners' ferocity with captured fugitives.[7]

Once Huck learns where Jim is, he undergoes his ultimate crisis of conscience, which concludes with his decision to risk hell to free Jim. So morally momentous is this decision that it seems Huck himself has developed morally.[8] In fact, though, if he is to develop morally, he must recognize the rightness of his decision, namely, that slavery, not abolition, is the sin; if he did, the novel's irony would evanesce.

Huck's crisis opens with a heartfelt yet remarkably conflicted statement: "After all this long journey, and after all we'd done for them scoundrels, here was it all come to nothing, everything all busted up and ruined, because they could have the heart to serve Jim such a trick as that, and make him a slave again all his life, and amongst strangers, too, for forty dirty dollars" (chap. 31). So, after the long journey, Huck finally acknowledges how terrible it is to be a slave. He recognizes no connection, though, between Jim's reenslavement and a journey that took him deeper and deeper into the South, nor between the scoundrels' sale of Jim and his own rebuff of Jim's plea to break with them. Instead, by implying that the long journey had a purpose for Jim when that purpose was lost in the fog, Huck hints both at his desire for Jim to stay with him on the raft and his aversion to helping Jim go free.

It is not difficult to discern a link between the rogues' sale of the Wilks slaves to strangers and Huck's express condemnation of the rogues for selling Jim "amongst strangers." However, given that one can object to such a sale and still uphold slavery, Huck's concern for a forlorn Jim is readily converted into an escape clause for Huck: since the rogues have consigned Jim to slavery among strangers, it would be a kindness if Huck arranged for him to be a slave among people he knows. But the steps Huck conceives to carry out this altruistic plan cancel each other out: he can let Miss Watson know where Jim is, but if Jim is sent back to her she will sell him down the river, and even if she doesn't, Jim will feel disgraced because "everybody naturally despises an ungrateful nigger" (chap. 31). Besides, it would get around that Huck Finn had helped free a "nigger" and his shame would be so great that if he ever ran across anyone from his town, he would get down and lick his boots. Of all those townspeople whose boots Huck might lick (and what if Mary Jane learned of his unpardonable sin?), he surely cannot conceive of a single one who would look down upon him with even a glimmer of the forgiveness that might be bestowed upon an ordinary penitent. (Somewhat oddly, perhaps, Huck fears only moral condemnation from other whites, thus overlooking the notorious legal and extralegal punishments that awaited if he were taken for an "Ablitionist.")[9]

It is only after Huck believes himself condemned on earth that he feels he is being watched from above. Realizing that he can hide nothing from Him, Huck submits to the dictates of conscience, writes his letter to Miss Watson, feels washed clean of sin, relieved that he will not be going to hell. Unfortunately, his pure intentions are subverted by his memories: Jim standing Huck's watch on top of his own, Jim welcoming him back out of the fog, Jim doing everything he can for Huck. The "nigger" has become Jim, and what Jim has performed are not services due Huck because he is white and Jim black, but acts of kindness from one human being to another.

When Huck condemns the rogues for selling Jim "after all we'd done for them," he censures them for substituting betrayal for what should have been gratitude. Thus a belief that kindness must be returned with kindness links his decision to risk hell for Jim with his decision to risk exposure by helping the Wilks sisters. Where one can be quite sure that Mary Jane's kindness to Huck influences his decision on Jim, one can only speculate as to whether hidden guilt over his implication in the fraud leading to the slaves' sale also plays a part. In any event, however humane Huck's decision to repay the debt of kindness he owes Jim, it is also inherently flawed: since he does not recognize Jim's right to be free, he resolves to rescue him by allowing personal considerations to override principle. Then, too, one personal consideration is uneasy with the other, given that a slaveowner's kindness to Huck influences his decision to rescue a fugitive slave.

Although Huck's decision regarding Jim is the converse of his stance with the Wilks slaves, a basic element in one crisis carries over to the other. While he confines the black family to the "nigger" slot, his subconscious doubts that they are subhuman creatures are a source of guilt; on the other hand, although he must release Jim from the "nigger" cage before he can decide to rescue him, the release is conditional, temporary. So long as "niggers" exist in Huck's mind, nothing he feels for Jim can prevent him from merging his friend with that invidious construct. Thus Huck's failed moral test with the enslaved black family foreshadows the precariousness of his commitment to Jim.

9 | The Kindness of Friends

I

Although nothing in *Huckleberry Finn* is quite as starkly white over black as its ending—whites threaten, imprison, shackle, torture, lie to, and pray over Jim—critics who assailed the ending, as well as those who defended it, failed to take note for almost seventy years. In 1885, Thomas Sergeant Perry criticized it because the "fun in the long account of Tom Sawyer's artificial imitations of escapes from prison is somewhat forced."[1] Fifty years later, Hemingway called *Huck Finn* "the best book we've had," while urging readers to skip the ending because it is "just cheating."[2] He offered no further explanation. And, in 1941, DeVoto's excoriation ("In the whole reach of the English novel there is no more abrupt or more chilling descent") was provoked by the belief that the ending is simply a "trivial extravaganza."[3] The severely limited or cryptic nature of this criticism explains why early defenses of the ending sound almost casual today. Take, for instance, Trilling's.

In retrospect it appears that Trilling was, if not exactly asking for trouble, perhaps a trifle rash when, after asserting that in "form and style *Huckleberry Finn* is an almost perfect work," he added: "Only one mistake has ever been charged against it, that it concludes with Tom Sawyer's elaborate, too elaborate, game of Jim's escape." He defended the ending on the grounds of "formal aptness."[4]

Trilling's assertion that only one mistake had ever been charged against *Huck Finn* became obsolete in 1953, when an analysis appeared that, John Reichert notes, "radically reinterpret[ed]" the novel by introducing "issues and episodes which [its] predecessors had overlooked."[5] With this reinterpretation, Jim was rescued from being the argument's invisible man: "The most serious motive in the novel, Jim's yearning for freedom, is made the object of nonsense," wrote Leo Marx. Miss Watson, "the Enemy," becomes Jim's liberator. Huck, who had "never found pain or misfortune amusing," becomes a "party to sport" that "aggravates Jim's misery." But "Jim doesn't mind too much. On the raft he was . . . man enough to denounce Huck when Huck made him the victim of a practical joke." Now when Jim is bitten by rats and snakes, "he bleeds ink and feels no pain"; he is "something less than human."[6] However, at the same time that Marx's critique radically reinterprets the ending, it also shares a characteristic of earlier critiques: it, too, divorces the ending from the rest of the book.

In fact, there is an integral connection between the ending and the preceding chapters. Early on, Jim puts his escape into the hands of a white boy with an aversion, at first subconscious, to going north with him. During the ending, Jim is compliant when his escape is taken over by another white boy, one who knows Jim's owner has freed her slave but who withholds that knowledge in order to defer the free man's freedom. That the deferral of Jim's freedom is a crucial link between the earlier chapters and the last ones was revealed by Toni Morrison: the "ending becomes the elaborate deferment of a necessary and necessarily unfree Africanist character's escape, because freedom has no meaning to Huck or to the text without the specter of enslavement."[7]

II

Morrison also points out, as we have noted, that Jim's presence is required for another reason as well: because there is "no way, given the confines of the novel, for Huck to mature into a moral human being *in America* without Jim." That keeping Jim with Huck is the only way provided Huck to develop morally does not mean (as is also evident from Morrison's analysis), however, that he does so develop.

When Huck, in search of Jim, arrives at the Phelps place, he finds Aunt Sally awaiting her nephew, Tom Sawyer. Mistaking Huck for Tom, she asks why he is so late in getting there.

> "We blowed out a cylinder head."
> "Good gracious! anybody hurt?"
> "No'm. Killed a nigger."
> "Well, it's lucky; because sometimes people do get hurt." (Chap. 32)

Most critics seem to agree that the irony in this exchange is strictly Twain's. Some, though, argue that Huck's reply is ironic, that he shrewdly tells Aunt Sally just what she will be glad to hear. If this view is accurate, Huck has broken his pattern of separating blacks from "people"; nothing sustains this. On the contrary, in this instance Huck uses "nigger" in a particularly aggressive way: since "No'm" answers Aunt Sally's question, his addition of the epithet is gratuitous. Gratuitous, that is, from Huck's standpoint, not from the author's. Whether or not this was Twain's conscious intent, the appended epithet is a reminder of why Huck, shortly after vowing to risk hell for Jim, can become a party to putting him through hell.

The author again places an ironic distance between himself and his narrator when, after Tom's arrival, Huck confesses that he is trying to "steal" Jim out of slavery. After Tom declares his eagerness to help, Huck is not only astonished that respectable Tom is ready (Huck believes) to bring shame upon himself and his family by becoming a *"nigger stealer,"* but also deeply disappointed: "I'm bound to say Tom Sawyer fell, considerable, in my estimation" (chap. 33). By having Huck reprise a sentiment he expresses when Jim, believing Cairo is near, reveals his plans to "steal" his children out of slavery ("I was sorry to hear Jim say that, it was such a lowering of him" [chap. 16]), Twain reminds the reader once more of the moral inversion that binds Huck to the belief that abolition is a sin.

Tom's eagerness to help free Jim is translated into a plan that calls for him to endure the trials of high-born prisoners in romance novels. So enamored is Tom with his escapade that he wishes he and Huck could keep up the fun of freeing Jim for "all the rest of our lives and leave Jim to our children to get out" (chap. 36). Huck is impressed with Tom's plan, but often argues against his time-consuming exactitude. Still, Huck's tone is disquieting even as he balks at replicating each detail prescribed by the "authorities": "When I start in to steal a nigger, or a watermelon, or a Sunday school book, I ain't no ways particular how it's done, so it's done. What I want is my nigger; or what I want is my watermelon; or what I want is my Sunday school book . . . and I don't give a dead rat what the authorities think about it, nuther" (chap. 36). Huck sounds rebellious, but his railing against authority, entwined as it is with racism, is more evocative of Pap denouncing the "govment" than of the boy who vowed to brave hell for Jim. Although this is not the first time Huck has referred to Jim with a possessive followed by "nigger," he now also explicitly equates him with objects. Huck further reveals his disdain by selecting for his analogy Sunday school books, which he wouldn't want if they were given to him, and watermelons. Authorial cues are hard to decipher here, given that Huck's disdain for Jim is masked as practical-minded opposition to Tom's romanticism, while laughter is invited by the proximity of "nigger" to "watermelon."

Perhaps Huck's behavior in these instances can be interpreted as the hardening of an often good-hearted but abidingly racist boy who feels bound to a commitment he was loath to make. But this alone cannot explain his delight after he and Tom infest Jim's cabin with snakes and rats: "You never see a cabin as blithesome as Jim's. . . . [W]hen the snakes was asleep the rats was on deck, and when the rats turned in the snakes come on watch, so he always had one gang under him . . . and t'other gang having a circus over him" (chap. 39). Nor can it explain Huck's glee after Tom hides a piece of brass in Jim's food: "it worked just noble: when Jim bit into it it most mashed all his teeth out" (chap. 36).

Huck never speaks directly of a change of heart toward Jim, but he has a special reason for acting so cruelly toward his companion of the river. Jim has told Uncle Silas Phelps that the duke and the king are about to put on a scandalous show. Huck rushes to warn the rogues, but word of their ruses has preceded them down the river and a raging mob is already riding them out of town on a rail. It is, Huck says, a dreadful sight: "Human beings *can* be awful cruel to one another." He could never again feel any hardness toward "them poor pitiful rascals"; he feels to blame somehow—"though *I* hadn't done nothing" (chap. 33).

Huck may say he feels to blame, but it is Jim he blames. Jim, whose role it is to forgive whites their trespasses, still feels a hardness toward the rascals merely because they sold him back into slavery. And he has done what no black man is allowed to do: evened the score with white men. Saintly, loving Jim has exacted vengeance—or, to be precise, uttered a few words and let white justice take its course. So, while the author's voice bids us admire Huck for his compassion (a successful bid, since Huck's remark about human cruelty is one of his most frequently quoted), it also murmurs that Jim is triply justified. Not only does Jim avenge himself, he also (wittingly or not) avenges the family the king put on the auction block. And he settles another score as well. Just before the rascals first board the raft, a black man saves the king's life by warning him that a mob is on the way. Thus when Jim tells, he evens things up with a rogue who repays one black person's kindness by selling four others.

Huck's changed attitude toward Jim lingers on. When he wants to get a doctor for Tom, who is wounded during the mock escape, he seems skeptical that Jim will want to risk his freedom by staying behind. Not only does Huck first "consult" with Jim, but he also prompts him: "Say it, Jim." Huck's concern, though, seems superfluous. Vowing to risk his freedom for Tom, Jim asks, rhetorically: if Tom were being set free and "one er de boys wuz to git shot," would Tom say, "save me, nemmine 'bout a doctor f'r to save dis one?" You can *bet* "mars Tom Sawyer" wouldn't. Having evoked his torturer as his model, Jim swears fidelity to him: "No, sah—I doan' budge a step out'n dis place, 'dout a *doctor;* not ef it's forty year!" (chap. 40). That Jim identifies himself as "one er de boys" reveals a self-image acquired from the black image in the white mind. Once a man with plans to bring his wife and children out of slavery, he is now too young even to think of a family. He is also young enough to assure the junior master forty more years of servitude. Bizarrely juvenilized, he is also grotesquely feminized. In a dress again when captured, he is praised by his captor, the doctor, for his faithfulness and exemplary nursing ("he ain't no bad nigger, gentlemen" [chap. 42]).

With Jim returned to his good graces (but not necessarily to a warm spot in his heart), Huck says: "I knowed he was white inside" (chap. 40). Supposedly praising him for acting like a white man (one wonders what model he has in mind), Huck actually praises Jim for acting as the society ordains for a black one—as a fount of endless love and sacrifice for whites. And, too, by according honorary whiteness to Jim retroactively, Huck also justifies his friendship with a fugitive slave, even suggests, perhaps, that, by being different from other blacks, Jim never deserved to be a slave.

III

Whatever their differences, most critiques of the ending that postdate Marx's have a common denominator: condemnation of its cruelty and its portrayal of Jim. For instance, E. L. Doctorow, after scoring the cruelty, states: "Huck Finn . . . struggles against the white mores of his time to help the black man, Jim, escape from slavery, but it is Huck's progenitor who portrays Jim, in minstrelese, as a gullible black child-man led by white children." He adds: "The irony may not be redemptive."[8] And Morrison writes: "Jim permits his persecutors to torment him, humiliate him, and responds to the torment and humiliation with boundless love."[9]

By contrast with the critiques of the ending, each type of defense is singular, one unrelated to another. James M. Cox, for instance, departs from the universal reading of *Huck Finn* as an attack on "social conscience," and sees it as an attack on conscience per se.[10] George C. Carrington, Jr., in a book-length defense, justifies the ending on structuralist grounds.[11] Forrest Robinson interprets Jim's compliance with his oppressors as his only possible hope for freedom.[12] Amid the many defenses, however, one has become dominant. It sees the ending as an allegory for the post-Reconstruction era when Twain was finishing the novel and when African-American rights were being forcibly deferred to an unforeseeable future. There are many variations of the ending-as-allegory view, but its essence is expressed in Eric J. Sundquist's version. Describing the last chapters as a "penetrating critique of the collapse of Reconstruction ideals," he writes:

> The "second slavery" of the nadir was . . . embedded in Twain's bitter humiliations of Jim . . . as Huck acquiesces in Tom's ludicrous imprisonment and parodic torment of a man already legally free. What ranks as one of the most notorious debates in the history of American literary criticism—the success or failure of the last chapters of *Huckleberry Finn*— . . . can be properly adjudicated only by reference to the renewed crisis over sectionalism and black rights that accompanied Twain's periods of composition. . . . "*Now*, old Jim, you're a free man *again*," says Huck, "and I bet you won't ever be a slave no more." At last finishing a draft of his famous novel in 1883, when the Supreme Court decided the landmark *Civil Rights Cases*, which cut the heart out of "equal protection" and led directly to *Plessy* [*v. Ferguson*], Twain knew otherwise.[13]

Sundquist's contention that the debate over the ending can be properly judged only by reference to events during the time in which Twain wrote it seems to suggest that if we recognize the allegory, we will see that it vindicates the ending. But should one have to step outside the novel's own time frame to make a just assessment of the ending? If the ending is to be taken as an allegory for another time, should it not be emblematic of its own?

As Sundquist notes, Huck acquiesces to Tom's plan for Jim's mock escape. But one should not overlook that Jim also acquiesces—even when it means letting the rats bite him so he can keep a "journal" in his own blood: "Jim he couldn't see no sense in the most of it, but he allowed we was white folks and knowed better than him" (chap. 36). One might agree with those who argue that Jim is putting on the boys, were it not that he *does* act as if white folks know better. Often unguarded and chained only to a bedpost, he could escape and turn to other blacks for help, but—displaying the traits that prompt the doctor to declare that he "ain't no bad nigger"—he stays put.

During slavery the archetypical "bad nigger" was Nat Turner, whose insurrection occurred in 1831 (just four years before the start of *Huck Finn*'s time frame). Curiously, the slave who brings Jim food is also called Nat. He is named that, observes Lott, "in what one can only assume is jocular homage to Nat Turner." Although Lott speaks of jocular homage, he treats the allusion to Turner as a serious matter: "Possessed of what Huck/Twain calls a 'good-natured, chuckle-headed face,' obsessed with fending off the witches he says have been haunting him, Nat is a sort of hysterical paranoiac." Lott also states that the "reference to Nat Turner's obsessive, visionary Christianity works to discredit both men." Raising the question of authorial voice, he concludes that the "very uncertainty of Twain's intentions, together with his seemingly happy blackface depiction of Nat's self-abasement, undercuts all but racist meanings from the scene."[14] Further comparison of Nat to Nat Turner reveals in the one a singular reversal of the other's traits: where Nat is a fool, Turner (in the words of a contemporary white) "evinced great intelligence";[15] where Nat is consumed by mindless fears, Turner was surpassingly courageous; where Nat's obsessive superstitions cause him to collapse in terror, Turner's religious visions fortified him for insurrection.[16]

When Twain was writing his novel, the white myths that arose during Reconstruction were not only active in their original form, but also on their way to being recycled by historians as scholarly judgments. Synthesizing these once-dominant views, Eric Foner states: "The white South . . . stood ready to do justice to the emancipated slaves," while the former slaves were either "passive victims of white manipulation" or "an unthinking people whose 'animal natures' threatened the stability of civilized society."[17] *Huck Finn*'s conflicted relation to these myths can be seen in the following:

On the one hand, the novel's white characters (with, one hopes, the exception of Huck) would never willingly do justice to blacks; on the other hand, its black characters would never threaten the "stability" of a white-dominated society. This antitraditionalist treatment of whites, accompanied by a traditionalist treatment of blacks, is particularly evident during the mock escape, which derides the white frenzy over black insurrection, but also derides black resistance.

The slaveowners' fear of insurrections reached irrational proportions, but it arose in the wake of real insurrections; Tom's game reduces Jim to a cipher, but causes the slaveowners to hallucinate that dozens of blacks are helping him escape. The farmers arm themselves and also threaten to lynch Jim. A farmer's wife exclaims: "Look at that shirt—every last inch of it kivered over with secret African writ'n, done with blood!" (chap. 41). (After Turner's papers were seized, they were found to contain hieroglyphical characters that appeared to be traced in blood.)[18] Thus, while the slaveowners may believe blacks are encoding dangerous messages, the reader knows it is Tom who decides what Jim will say, blocks out the letters, and—capping a portrait analogous to that of the ex-slaves as passive victims of white manipulation—leaves him "nothing to do but just follow the lines" (chap. 38).

If one considers only the behavior of the whites during the ending, one might agree with the critic Sherwood Cummings, who holds that the ending "satirize[s] the principle and practice of white supremacy."[19] In reality, though, it is impossible to satirize/subvert the myth of white supremacy while reiterating the myths of black gullibility, passivity, dependency, and so forth.

IV

As revisionist historians have long since shown, the ex-slaves were not apolitical pawns, but central to the effort to construct a new social order. "Rather than passive victims of the actions of others . . . blacks were active agents in the making of Reconstruction," observes Foner, who also states: "Prodded by the demands of four million men and women just emerging from slavery, Americans made their first attempt to live up to the noble professions of their political creed. . . . The effort produced a sweeping redefinition of the nation's public life and a violent reaction that ultimately destroyed much, but by no means all, of what had been accomplished."[20]

Between 1867 and 1877, two thousand black men held offices ranging from member of Congress to justice of the peace.[21] Albion Tourgée, a Reconstruction judge, said of the African-American voters: "They instituted a public school system in a realm where public schools had been unknown. They opened the ballot-box and jury box to thousands of white men who had been debarred from them by a lack of earthly possessions. . . . They abolished the whipping post and branding iron, the stocks and other barbarous forms of punishment which up to that time prevailed. . . . In an age of extravagance they were extravagant in the sums appropriated for public works."[22]

The violence against blacks that began during Reconstruction was aimed at driving them out of office. "The real stimulus . . . to the growth and expansion of Klan activities was . . . the apparent determination on the part of blacks and their Radical [Republican] friends to assume and wield political power," states John Hope Franklin.[23] An incident that occurred in Hamburg, South Carolina, in 1876 illustrates why it took the Ku Klux Klan and at least ten other violent white supremacist organizations,[24] abetted by the withdrawal of federal troops, to end Reconstruction: "The black militia, parading in observance of Independence Day, was ordered from the streets; and when they failed to obey, they were arrested. At their trial, armed groups of whites came into the court to see that the blacks received 'justice.' When they refused to apologize and surrender their arms, the whites fired on them, killing five. Others were killed as they attempted to flee. This and other disorders set the stage for the election in which [ex-Confederate general] Wade Hampton [became governor]."[25] Resistance such as this could hardly metamorphose into acquiescence in the next era. In fact, African Americans "never acknowledged the justice of the social order under which they were forced to live," notes Foner.[26] Instead, they "resist[ed] within the limits of their power," states Herbert Shapiro.[27]

For instance, in 1879 hundreds of African Americans emigrated from Mississippi, Louisiana, Texas, and Tennessee to Kansas, which "in the black consciousness . . . symbolized cheap land and also the antislavery struggle led by John Brown." Once there, they were confronted by whites who believed the land should be for whites only.[28] In 1883 blacks in Virginia were allied in a statewide election with white farmers and small businessmen against wealthy citizens and state officials. Just before the election, three blacks were killed in Danville. Blacks there petitioned Washington (unsuccessfully) for federal troops to be sent in on election day. Elsewhere in the state, blacks paraded; later they guarded the polls. But white supremacists, via racial demagoguery and violence, emerged the victors.[29] And in 1883 in Copiah County, Mississippi, black voters united with a large number of the poorer white ones; "together they revived the Reconstruction experiment."[30] Shortly before election day, armed planters and other highly placed whites raided black precincts, threatening to kill blacks known to be active politically. A black farmer and his wife were murdered. In the face of threats, both blacks and whites hid out in the woods. The violence climaxed on election day with the murder of a prominent merchant-planter, who was a Republican. Many African Americans were among those who testified to the violence at U.S. Senate hearings in New Orleans.[31] In 1887, black sugar workers in Louisiana struck against conditions of neo-slavery. The governor sent in troops to suppress the strike; strikers were arrested and murdered; white mobs added to the violence. Blacks, supported by the Knights of Labor, demanded an investigation, but the strike was "broken by official violence."[32] And in 1892, Homer Plessy, a light-skinned African American—taking the first step in the journey that would lead from the Supreme Court's notorious "separate but equal" ruling in *Plessy v. Ferguson* in 1896 to the ruling's overturn in *Brown v. Board of Education* in 1954—sat down in a whites-only car in an intrastate Louisiana train, announced he was a Negro, and was arrested.[33]

The dates in these incidents range from the time when Twain was writing *Huckleberry Finn* to the time when it was in the hands of its early readers. Whether these readers saw in its white characters—slaveowners, slavetraders, et al.—their post-Reconstruction analogues is questionable; in all probability, they could easily relegate such types to an increasingly misted past. But they were surely ready to accept Jim, who is "pleased most to death" when Tom gives him forty dollars for being such a good prisoner (chap. the last), as representative of the former slaves and their descendants.

V

Whatever else the ending of *Huckleberry Finn* may be—biting allegory or chilling descent, satire or farce, or some surreal mix thereof—it is the story of the end of American literature's most renowned black-white friendship. The signal that, so far as Huck is concerned, it is over is buried in his most mythologized remark: "But I reckon I got to light out for the Territory ahead of the rest, because aunt Sally she's going to adopt me and sivilize me and I can't stand it. I been there before" (chap. the last).

Many allusions have been discovered in Huck's desire to light out ahead of "the rest," but in context it has a specific meaning: Tom is the first to speak of the territory; he wants to go there with Huck and Jim for howling adventures. Although Tom is almost well, Huck does not care to wait. Nor does the vagueness of his destination suggest a future reunion. Huck no longer confides his feelings to his readers. But if they have changed toward Tom, it is understandable, since Huck now knows Tom tricked him by withholding his knowledge that Jim had been freed.

The "rest," though, also includes Jim, whose availability Huck does not attempt to determine. He now also knows that Jim tricked him by concealing that the dead man was Pap. Huck may have forgotten Jim's fear that, if Huck were free to go home, Huck might betray him. But even if he remembered, it would make no difference; Huck's reactions when he thinks himself bested by Jim in their verbal battles suggest that he would consider being tricked by a black man a breach of the natural order. (Huck seems unconcerned that Tom tricked Jim, but then Jim is delighted with Tom's forty-dollar compensation.) Although this seems reason enough to explain why Huck wishes to go without Jim, Huck's feelings for Jim appear to wane long before he learns that Jim tricked him.

On the raft, the often emotionally and physically famished Huck needs Jim's love, faithfulness, and food. When he arrives at the Phelps place, Huck reenters white society, is sated with food, and, above all, reunited with Tom. In a novel noted for its "doubling," or paired incidents, Twain uses this means to signal Huck's reimmersion in a sanctioned world: while Jim is confined with the rats and snakes, Huck relives the river idyll, only this time with Tom; the two spend a perfect day fishing and eating on the Mississippi.

As for the territory, perhaps Huck *is* planning to go to there because Aunt Sally expects to "adopt me and sivilize me." But if the reason he gives is his reason for going, we too have been there before. On the other hand, he may have learned that it is easier and more comfortable to tell people what they want to hear. If he says he is running away from constricting women, he can anticipate indulgence; if he says he is running away from mayhem, murder, and slavery (if only because it has imperiled him, body and soul), he declares, dangerously, that he is running away from the society itself.

Huck's story comes to an end, but our debate continues over how far, or in which direction, he has traveled since the time he exclaims to Jim, "They're after us!" Even if we conclude that he now finds it more comfortable to observe racial proscriptions, we may still hope. After all, if he is young enough to believe he will find in the territory whatever he is looking for, surely he is still young enough to change. Or is he? After all, the victory of his kind heart over his deformed conscience was fleeting. And, too, change would largely depend on the friends he makes among the strangers he encounters. If these thoughts shadow our optimism, it may be that we expected too much of him in the first place. If so, we should not blame Huck for failing to live up to our expectations, but remember instead that he is America's child.

Fault Lines

I

On September 25, 1957, eleven days after the Arkansas National Guard stopped them from entering Central High, nine black students, now shielded by federal troops, walked through its doors. On September 25, 1997, the former students returned to Central High to commemorate its desegregation. The main speaker for the occasion was the president, who said, "Segregation is no longer the law, but too often separation is still the rule." He also stated: "For the first time since the 1950's, our schools . . . are resegregating." But, the *New York Times* pointed out, "he offered no programmatic solutions" for the schools or beyond. Instead, he appeared to leave the matter to the consciences of whites: "After all the weary years and silent tears, . . . the stony roads and bitter rods, the question of race is, in the end, still an affair of the heart."[1]

Although it would be difficult to contend that change at Central High was brought about by changed hearts, those who fought for desegregation undoubtedly helped change some of those who resisted it.[2] Change, though, has gone just so far. Like many other schools across the country, Central High is statistically desegregated but otherwise largely divided by race.[3]

II

The fortieth anniversary of the desegregation of Central High also marked the fortieth year of a related event, the controversy over *Huck Finn*'s place in the schools. Perhaps the debate's most striking feature at this point was the degree to which it had remained in a time warp. For instance, in responding to the criticisms of Jim in 1957, the *Times* editorial pointed out that his goodness causes Huck to tear up his letter to Miss Watson. Today, basically the same reason is given to defend *Huck Finn*'s place on the curriculum. A current version, though, goes much beyond the *Times*'s accurate description of Jim's effect on Huck. Nat Hentoff asserts: "Look at that Huck Finn. Reared in racism, like all the white kids in his town. And then, on the river, on the raft with Jim, shucking off that blind ignorance because this runaway slave is the most honest, perceptive, fair-minded man this white boy has ever known. What a book for the children, all the children!"[4] If children are taught that Huck casts off his racism, the lesson, or tale, should begin "Once upon a time, there was a boy named Huck. . . . " Hard as it may be to acknowledge enduring racism in a legendary character (much more comfortable to confine it to a depraved Pap), arguing otherwise is to maintain that it was possible to overcome racist beliefs while continuing to accept slavery.

Although the contention that Huck casts off his racism because Jim is an exemplar seems to credit Jim with Huck's presumed transformation, in fact it subtly transfers the onus for whites' views of blacks to blacks; it implies that through association with exemplary blacks, whites will overcome their preexisting attitudes—thus overlooking that white attitudes arise from historical misperceptions of blacks. Of course, a friendship with a black person (who need not be a paragon) may lead a white person to question old assumptions, thus becoming a step toward his or her recognition of the human equality of blacks. On the other hand, a white with a black friend may be unable to let go of traditional beliefs about race and instead try to fit the black friend into them. This is just what Huck does when he praises Jim with the words "I knowed he was white inside."[5]

In 1860, Douglass pointed out that relations between individual blacks and whites are far more than a personal matter: "Consciously or unconsciously, almost every white man approaches a colored man with an air of superiority and condescension. The relation subsisting between the races at once shows itself between the individuals."[6] Since Douglass speaks of "almost every white man," it is evident that he encountered relatively few white abolitionists who acted differently in this respect from other whites. (While it was impossible to accept slavery and overcome racism, it was all too possible to oppose slavery and retain racist notions.)[7]

Even if Huck, taught to accept slavery and abhor abolitionists, had encountered a fugitive slave comparable to those of history, he might have retained his original views of blacks; on the other hand, there would have been a credible basis for his changing. But a Jim who lacks the potential for influencing white readers to question stereotypes cannot be expected to help transform Huck. If we assess Huck as if he were a human being, his worth is lessened by his remaining racist; if we assess him as a character, this is not necessarily so. If his significance is predicated on authenticity rather than transformation, it is undiminished by his failure to change. But his significance in this sense is compromised by the distracting authorial cues that disguise his racist behavior, particularly as comedy. All in all, these diversionary signals overwhelm those which Twain provides when he wants his readers to see Huck's conduct and beliefs for what they are. So the problem is not that Huck remains racist, but that Twain either does not recognize instances of Huck's racism, or does not want the reader to.[8]

Critics who argue that Huck's relationship with Jim transforms the boy seem to find encouragement in one of Ellison's remarks: "Twain fitted Jim into the outlines of the minstrel tradition, and it is from behind this stereotype mask that we see Jim's dignity and human capacity—and Twain's complexity—emerge." These critics appear to overlook Ellison's next lines: "Yet it is his source in this same tradition which creates that ambivalence between his identification as an adult and parent and his 'boyish' naivete, and which by contrast makes Huck, with his street-sparrow sophistication, seem more adult. Certainly it upsets a Negro reader."[9] No matter what virtues Jim may have, none can compensate for the fact that—in this iconic white-black relationship—the white boy appears more adult, that is, more intelligent, than the black man.

The novel's treatment of Huck and Jim also has converse implications for class and ethnic assumptions as compared to racial ones. Huck, a poor boy from a then-maligned ethnic group, could—with his quick wits, daring improvisations, and ceaseless searching—rise quickly to become America's child. But Jim—with traits that invert Huck's—could never transcend in a reader's imagination the "place" that, at the time *Huck Finn* was published, the society had preordained for African-American adults.

III

Another problem in teaching *Huck Finn* that has remained in a time warp since 1957 is the novel's use of the racial epithet. For instance, in the 1980s, in a Pennsylvania town where black parents had challenged the book, a school official expressed exasperation with them for criticizing the usage: "Good Lord, Twain spends three-quarters of his book trying to make clear what a damnable word 'nigger' is, because it shows the whites who used it didn't *see*, didn't begin to understand the people they were talking about."[10] Thus, according to this, the explanation for its characters' use of "nigger" lies within *Huck Finn.* That *Huck Finn* does not support this view is inadvertently confirmed by those who offer blanket defenses of the usage.

For example, critics and educators who justify the epithet as antebellum vernacular and a synonym for "slave" have not explained why "nigger" rather than "slave" is the novel's preferred term, nor provided evidence that it was simply idiomatic, let alone shown when in our history "nigger" was converted from vernacular to debasing. Nor have they taken note that their view of the word as idiomatic is contradicted by the other major justification: that Twain recognized the word as derogatory and used it for ironic purposes. At the same time, however, those who support the latter view have not considered the possibility of a gap between what may have been Twain's intent and what he realized.

Despite the fact that their justifications conflict, the defenders maintain that blacks who criticize the novel's use of the epithet simply fail to get the point. This contention reverses a history in which African Americans have compelled whites to face up to the meaning of "nigger"—have, in fact, made it impossible for whites who use it to claim they mean nothing derogatory. At the same time, blacks have shown themselves to be masters of the ironic use of the epithet. In an essay written in the early 1940s, W. E. B. Du Bois pointed out that "nigger" assumed a variety of sophisticated, satirical meanings when used by blacks among themselves. However, he also classified it as a word "no white man must use." One may be inclined to think he was speaking of oral, not literary usage, but he chose to publish this view in the *Mark Twain Quarterly*.[11]

Given that Du Bois presented a general rule, let us consider a potential exception: a white author who puts the word in the mouths of white characters while also conveying to the reader that it is a word no white should use. At times Twain suggests this, as when he traces Huck's mercurial feelings for Jim through the boy's shifts from "nigger" to "Jim" and vice versa. But the novel's overall use of the epithet is so casually repetitive that only readers who consider each appearance on its own terms will identify the ironic ones. Thus, while the novel's use of the epithet might serve as a transcript of white dialogue in that time and place, from a literary standpoint repetition overwhelms function (Quirk speaks of Twain's "excessive, perhaps obsessive use of the word *nigger*").[12]

Those who maintain that *Huck Finn*'s use of "nigger" is clearly ironic also fail to note that the black characters use it—not among themselves, but when speaking to whites—as casually as the white ones. Does the blacks' use of the word support the claim that it was simply vernacular? Within the novel's parameters, there is no answer. Or is the blacks' usage ironic because they themselves did not recognize the word as degrading? This may easily be inferred from *Huck Finn*. What one cannot guess is that when slaves used the epithet in the presence of whites, they did so as a defense: had they shunned it, their owners would have regarded their speech as insolent and treated them accordingly.[13]

As we have noted, when critics attempted to rebut the objections to *Huck Finn,* they projected it in a new way, that is, as a work primarily of importance for its treatment of slavery and race. The schools followed suit, with educators emphasizing its value as a means for teaching antebellum history. For instance, in the Pennsylvania district where the novel was being challenged, the same school official maintained that it "ties in very well with the pre–Civil War history" that most ninth graders study.[14] As this and remarks from other educators suggest, many, if not most, teachers fail to distinguish between passages that have an authentic, albeit not necessarily literal, connection with history (the one, say, where Huck's conscience prods him to turn Jim over to the slaveowners) and passages that retell myths (the one, say, where Jim risks his chance to rescue his own family to save a white boy who has plagued him). Nor is there any evidence that educators generally take note of the singular direction of Jim's escape.

Huck Finn's asserted reliability as history is also used to defend it against challenges—with predictable results. For instance, in answer to a questionnaire in a college class, most of the fifty white students maintained that "the novel gives a historically accurate picture of slavery and thus should be immune from criticism." And while all of the fifty white students held that "there was nothing whatever in *Huckleberry Finn* to offend any rational, fair-minded person," all six of the black students declared the opposite.[15]

IV

Those who equate the black challengers of *Huck Finn* as required reading with the Concord moralists and contemporary fundamentalists overlook essential differences. While moralists and fundamentalists claim to act on behalf of children in proscribing *Huck Finn,* it is black children themselves who object to the indignities that accompany classroom readings of the novel. And their objections are to being humiliated both as individuals and as members of a racial group.

These points are generally lost in the media treatment of the controversy, which has focused in particular on John H. Wallace, a former school administrator. While carefully substantiated criticisms of the novel receive minimal attention, Wallace—who characterizes it as "the most grotesque example of racist trash ever written"[16]—has been interviewed, appeared on TV talk shows, and frequently quoted by the novel's champions. Cautioning against the use of his statements to dismiss the challengers' concerns, the Twain scholar Quirk—his deep admiration for *Huck Finn* notwithstanding—says: "Wallace may overstate his case at times, but that should not divert us from the fact that he does have a case to make."[17] Wallace makes a case when, for instance, he tells of his first encounter, as one of two black children in an otherwise all-white class, with the book: "Every time the teacher, reading it aloud, mentioned the word 'nigger,' I flinched. . . . [E]very time [the other black child] heard the teacher say that word, he put his head down on the desk."[18]

Allen B. Ballard, a professor of political science, is among those who tell of similar experiences: "I remember vividly the experience of having read *Huck Finn* in a predominantly white junior high school in Philadelphia some thirty years ago. I can still recall the anger and pain I felt as my white classmates read aloud the word 'nigger.' In fact, as I write . . . I am getting angry all over again." Ballard asks: "Why should a learning experience, intended to make children love literature, instead end up inflicting pain upon Black children?"[19]

Another incident is related by the poet Sonia Sanchez, who noticed a "very strange look" on her son's face when his junior high school class was reading *Huck Finn*. "I feel that Jim is not a human being," her son, Mungu, said, adding that Jim was there only to serve whites. At his mother's suggestion, Mungu took the matter up with his teacher, who replied that "a lot of Blacks were not intelligent at the time the book was written, and they were too ignorant to understand how they were being treated." Mungu answered: "Blacks were powerless, not unintelligent."[20]

Remembrances of *Huck Finn* in the classroom have also made their way into a place where the most lasting memories surface, the autobiographical novel. In *High Cotton*, by Darryl Pinckney, black students, before the birthday of Martin Luther King, Jr., was made a national holiday, stay away from school on the anniversary of his death. The narrator, whose consciousness has not caught up with theirs, does not. But after coming to school, he "walked out of class rather than relive the indignities of *The Adventures of Huckleberry Finn*."[21]

When Pinckney speaks of the indignities of *Huckleberry Finn*, he is in a literal sense speaking of the indignities inherent in the novel. These intrinsic indignities may, though, be exacerbated in the classroom to the point where the novel per se becomes indistinguishable from or subsumed by the affronts. By contrast, some children who first read the novel on their own—imaginations unencumbered, free to linger wherever they wish—may distinguish among its various facets. For instance, when Toni Morrison read it on her own, she found it different from other books on the "children's shelf": "at no point along Huck's journey was a happy ending signaled or guaranteed."[22]

Morrison's second reading took place in junior high school. This one "provoked a feeling I can only describe now as muffled rage, as though appreciation of the work required my complicity in and sanction of something shaming." Presiding over the class was a teacher who allowed the epithet—with the "offense Mark Twain's use" of it causes black children, and its "corrosive effect" on white ones—to go unremarked. "A serious comprehensive discussion of the term by an intelligent teacher certainly would have benefited my eighth-grade class and would have spared all of us (a few blacks, many whites . . .) some grief." Instead, the children heard "the dread word spoken, and therefore sanctioned, in class." Despite this, Morrison found new satisfactions in her second reading, including "riveting episodes of flight, of cunning," and "convincing commentary on adult behavior."[23]

V

In the years since it became required reading, most children have met *Huck Finn* only in the classroom. And by the 1970s and 1980s, it had been required reading long enough to create what one parent describes as two generations of pain: "My adventure with *Huckleberry*

Finn has been a stinging and bitter one, one which has left a dull pain that spans two generations, mine and my son's," relates Margot Allen.[24]

In 1957, Allen was the only black student in her ninth-grade class. As the class got into the novel, "the dialect alone made me feel uneasy." She pretended not to be bothered by "that awful word": "I hid, from my teacher and my classmates, the tension, discomfort and hurt I would feel every time I heard that word or watched the class laugh at Jim." The hardest part was keeping her composure while others stared. "Somehow I thought that a blank face would protect me from not only this book's offensiveness and open insults, but the silent indicting, accusing and sometimes apologetic stares of my classmates." A quarter of a century later, Allen's son, the only African American in his ninth-grade English class, was asked by the teacher to read the part of Jim. "He has the perfect voice for it," she said. Students laughed. "My son was humiliated, though he, too, tried to hide his feelings." After class, some students were supportive, but others "took the opportunity to snicker 'nigger' under their breath to him." Allen visited the teacher, who asserted that other black students had been "proud" to read Jim's lines. Allen, the academic coordinator for Penn State's Office of Academic Assistance Program, took many other steps to resolve the matter positively, but without success. "Whatever the book's merits," she states, "there is a cost to pay in reading it, and unfortunately that cost is borne in large part by young Black students. . . . There is also a cost to white students, whose out-dated notions of white superiority are reinforced."[25]

Among those authors, critics, and educators who sympathize with the black parents' concerns over *Huck Finn* in the classroom, there is a diversity of opinion on what to do. For instance, the novelist and professor of English Julius Lester states: "I am grateful that among the many indignities inflicted on me in childhood, I escaped *Huckleberry Finn*. As a black parent, however, I sympathize with those who want the book banned, or at least removed from required reading lists in schools. While I am opposed to book banning, I know that my children's education will be enhanced by not reading *Huckleberry Finn*."[26] By contrast, despite the unpleasant aspects of her classroom encounter with the novel, Morrison believes that this "amazing, troubling book" should remain there.[27]

Stephen Railton also believes it should stay on the curriculum: "The reason to make it required reading is that it is the perfect occasion to confront the meaning and consequences of racism. . . . Indeed, since it is racist as well as about racism, it is part of the problem. The vexed aptness of *Huck Finn* is that it makes the problem immediate, personal, emotionally compelling."[28] And Kay Puttock, a college teacher, states, "Educators today are teaching in classrooms filled with simmering racial prejudice and tension." Although she has "met high school teachers who refuse to teach it," Puttock believes it can be taught effectively.[29]

But Marylee Hengstebeck, also a college teacher, decided not to teach it: "I love *Huck Finn,* always have, and while I accept the fact that it's racist, it's also many other things—breezy, hilarious, complex." But one factor in particular tipped the scales in Hengstebeck's decision not to teach it: "I had no idea how ugly ['nigger'] sounds read aloud nor the charged atmosphere that results from it. Listening to black students tell me firsthand how it made them feel is what changed my mind."[30]

An early instance of an educator deciding not to teach *Huck Finn* occurred at the University of Chicago in the 1960s, when the only African-American member of the humanities teaching staff, Paul Moses, said he found the portrayal of Jim so offensive that he became angry in class and was unable to make the white students understand why. Nor did he think it right, he also said, to subject students, black or white, to the novel's distorted views of race. The other staff members, who included the critic Wayne Booth, were shocked. Although they granted Moses's request not to teach it, they continued to believe he was wrong. "I can remember lamenting the shoddy education that had left poor Paul Moses unable to recognize a great classic when he met one," recalls Booth. Although Booth would "resist anyone who tried to ban the book from *my* classroom," he came to believe that Moses's reading of the novel, "an overt ethical appraisal, is one legitimate form of literary criticism."[31]

Arac expresses still another view of *Huck Finn* as a classroom text:

"If *Huckleberry Finn* were read and taught only for pleasure, there would be much less passion in defending its classroom role." Arac says this in his introduction, but near the end of his book he seems to take issue with his own counsel. Questioning whether pleasure in an aesthetic sense can triumph over pain in a historical one, he asks: "What can assure that the pain does not overwhelm the pleasure? The continuing present vividness of America's historical racism is what provokes the pain that leads students and their parents to protest the classroom prestige of *Huckleberry Finn*."[32]

VI

In a classic debate, there is mutual agreement on the terms; in the *Huck Finn* debate, one side set them. By obliterating the difference between banning *Huck Finn* and discontinuing it as required reading, the dominant side defined the debate as one between censors and champions of free speech. This side also erased the debate's other distinctive characteristics—including the fact that it was initiated by children. Not all critics, however, have accepted the prevailing definition. "First Amendment pleadings that serve to exonerate or extenuate Twain and his novel are beside the point," declares Quirk.[33] Leo Marx also rejects the portrayal of the debate as one between free speech advocates and censors: "Unlike most issues of public policy involving opposed literary judgments, the current argument about the place of *Huckleberry Finn* in the public school curriculum does not involve censorship or First Amendment rights. Whether or not high-school students are required to read a particular novel has nothing to do with anyone's freedom of speech." Marx sharply distinguishes between the challenge to *Huck Finn* as required reading and the demand (which has been made only rarely) to remove it from libraries ("I am putting aside the very different and, to my mind, intolerable proposal to remove the book from school or public libraries").[34] After inquiring as to whether Jim's one "splendid moment" in rebuking Huck is "splendid enough" to offset his "customary pliancy," Marx continues:

To raise these complex issues, it need hardly be said, is not to condone the denunciation of the novel as racist trash. But even if that opinion is as wrongheaded as I believe it to be, it does not follow that those who hold it are necessarily wrong about the inappropriateness of requiring high-school teachers to teach, and students to read, the *Adventures of Huckleberry Finn.* The point at issue, then, is the justification for that requirement. To claim that it should be required reading because it is a great American book is unconvincing; we don't require students to read most great books.[35]

First Amendment defenses of *Huck Finn* as mandatory reading oddly overlook that this condition requires teachers to teach it. Marx, however, believes they should be allowed to decide whether or not to teach it. Carey-Webb agrees: "No teacher should be required to teach this novel." He stipulates a further condition: "we need to listen to objections raised to the novel, [and] reconsider the *process* of teaching it."[36]

For decades, school officials and teachers have nominally heard the objections, but few have *listened.* However, not only are white administrators and teachers typically reluctant to listen to objections from blacks, but they are also aware of the media reaction that follows any effort to meet black concerns. For example, after his class read *Huckleberry Finn,* a black eighth grader was taunted with "nigger" and also reported to have suffered physical abuse. Responding to protests by black parents, the school officials changed the novel's status from required reading in junior high to a book that teachers could choose to teach at the high school level. Typifying the media response to any compromise on this matter, Hentoff wrote that the white school officials "had shown themselves to be sensitive to the feelings of this very small minority in the district (about two hundred black kids out of eleven thousand students)."[37] Hentoff quite explicitly expresses what is usually an implicit justification for rejecting African-American parents' concerns over *Huck Finn:* that a minority's objections threaten to deprive the majority of a valuable learning experience in race relations. That whites acquire something worthwhile from classroom events that humiliate and anger blacks (or would if they were present) is a singular notion. It is, though, consistent with the fact that white students' supposed reactions are taken as normative for the entire student population—in this instance, taken as evidence that black students' and parents' call for a change in the novel's status as required reading may be dismissed.

At the same time that the schools' resistance to such criticism has been painful to black students, it has had a desensitizing effect on white ones. The "aura of controversy" around *Huck Finn* has had "a long-lasting negative effect on some white students' literary sensitivity and even on their ordinary humanity," Puttock relates. "It seems that by the time many students get to college they have become so habituated to hearing a book like *Huckleberry Finn* defended from even the suspicion of censorship, that their literary, critical and even ethical faculties go into abeyance whenever it is discussed."[38]

Although, as we have noted, there has been some support from white faculty members and administrators to the challenges to *Huckleberry Finn* from black parents and students, apparently no white parents or students have initiated analogous ones. That this is interpreted as reassuring instead of a cause for concern is hardly an unprecedented phenomenon. After all, assertions that all goes well with race relations have historically come from whites, no matter how distinct the signals from blacks to the contrary. Still, white dissenters are also a part of history, and we may assume the presence of some when *Huck Finn* is taught. But unlike their black classmates, whites have not recorded their memories of studying the novel in a desegregated setting. A few white adults have, however, written of their feelings after they abdicated a traditional interpretation of the novel. One of them is Wayne Booth, whose experience with Paul Moses began to turn his perception of *Adventures of Huckleberry Finn* "once and for all" from "untroubled admiration to restless questioning. And," Booth concludes, "it is a kind of questioning that Twain and I alone together could never have managed for ourselves."[39]

If Twain—on his own, a century earlier—had written the antiracist novel that many of his current champions insist he wrote, the uproar at its publication would have been of quite a different sort from the one we may laugh away today. When the Concord moralists acted to protect children from *Huckleberry Finn* as rough, coarse, and inelegant, Twain was not displeased. Their ban would, he knew, sell books. He could not, of course, foresee that in the future children would be required to read the book whose child-narrator flees adult coercion. Nor could he have imagined that disapproval of his novel would come one day from black children. Those who brush aside these children's pain and protests no doubt believe they defend Twain's legacy, may even believe they speak on his behalf. We do Twain a grave injustice, though, if we presume he would agree.

Afterword

A belief, probably widespread, exists that the color line at the entrance to the national cultural conversation, so glaring in 1941 when a critic chose a parlor as the metaphorical site, has vanished. There are, though, not-infrequent indications to the contrary. For instance, in the 1990s two political scientists pointed out that in many "leading works on racial attitudes in the United States, black people are conspicuous largely by their absence." Why the absence of African Americans? "The first answer is simply that it has long been considered more important to understand whites' attitudes than blacks'."[1]

If blacks' opinions have been considered dispensable to in-depth studies on racial attitudes, they are now often considered essential to instant surveys. Whether these polls, which frequently show most blacks and most whites clustered on racial questions at opposite ends of a statistical curve, have helped us understand either whites' or blacks' attitudes is questionable. One inference from the racial rifts, statistical and otherwise, that has gained currency is that blacks and whites know little about each other and must overcome mutual ignorance. It is true that separation fosters mythology on both sides of the gap, but it is inaccurate to assert an equality of ignorance. The phenomenon that arose during slavery still persists: those of the socially disfavored racial group are compelled to learn about those of the socially preferred one, while the latter have no such incentive. Not only do blacks know far more about whites than whites know about blacks, but they also know things about whites that whites themselves do not know. That blacks surely were not surprised that their criticism of *Huckleberry Finn* evoked shocked white resistance simply illustrates the point.

The black challenges to *Huckleberry Finn* elicit particularly strong opposition because of the novel's unique identification with the American dream. In fact, though, the novel does not express *the* American dream, which is as illusory as *the* great American novel. Rather, Huck's dream has an affinity to that of immigrants, whose lives here often fell short of their imaginings. Although many continued to harbor their dreams, most did not act on them; the same often held true for their descendants. Huck not only acts on his dream, he fulfills it, and its realization—the raft floating down the great river—has evoked nostalgia in generations of readers. His resolve, after his raft utopia is destroyed, to seek his dream in "the Territory" has also generated powerful feelings of identification. The desire to attain one's dream is universal, but Huck's dream—expressed as masculine opposition to what he perceives as feminine constraints, while tacitly assuming the absence of freedom for blacks—is bounded by color and gender.

While immigrants came with a preconceived American dream of freedom, blacks, whose loss of freedom was the condition of their arrival, created a dream of freedom *in* America. Twain recognized that blacks had their own dreams, and early on, Jim expresses his. But Jim's dream is soon subordinated to Huck's, and then, as the raft drifts ever further downstream, is lost. And when, finally, paperthin freedom is bestowed upon him, he declares himself satisfied. Thus Twain either did not realize or did not wish to suggest that the African-American dream—an overarching social dream encompassing myriads of personal ones—had long been stubbornly held and, in one way and another, relentlessly pursued.

Within the controversy over *Huck Finn,* there are both highly visible and half-obscured conflicts: one person's nostalgia may be another's bitter memories; one person may identify with Huck's dream, while another may feel excluded from it; one person's laughter may be another's pain and anger; one may see in Huck and Jim exemplars of black-white friendship, while another sees familiar images of racial difference. The intensity and longevity of these clashes are a compelling reminder that the *Huckleberry Finn* controversy is not only over fictional black-white relations, but also—or, rather, primarily—over real ones.

Notes

Introduction

1. Kenneth Burke, *The Philosophy of Literary Form: Studies in Symbolic Action* (Baton Rouge: Louisiana State University Press, 1941), 110–11.

Chapter 1: The Trespassers

1. The governor was Orville Faubus. The NAACP leader was Daisy Bates, who, with her husband, published the *State Press*, an African-American weekly newspaper. Bates, who had established a local reputation in the struggle for equal rights, became nationally known for her role in the Little Rock episode. Our retelling of the incident is based on the account in Herbert Shapiro, *White Violence and Black Response: From Reconstruction to Montgomery* (Amherst: University of Massachusetts Press, 1988), 411–17.

2. The student was Elizabeth Eckford; the *Times* education editor, Benjamin Fine; the white woman who intervened was Grace Lorch, a professor at Philander Smith College; Dwight D. Eisenhower was president.

3. Leonard Buder, "*Huck Finn* Barred as Textbook by City," *New York Times,* September 12, 1957, pp. 1, 29.

4. Ibid., 29. The comment, which Buder paraphrases, was made by Ethel Huggard, associate school superintendent in charge of curriculum development.

5. The *Times* reporter also spoke to an unidentified official of an unnamed publisher (actually Scott, Foresman & Co.), who said his company had been told that its contract for the book was not being renewed because the novel contained "some passages derogatory to Negroes." The edition replaced "nigger"

with "negro," and was criticized for not capitalizing the latter (ibid.). (The edition also revised *Huckleberry Finn* in other ways.) Since this adaptation was published in 1951, it appears that criticism of *Huck Finn*'s use of the epithet was registered considerably before the incident in 1957. What, if any, effect this criticism had on the board of education is unclear, since only one of the four editions in use in the city's schools was reported to have excised the epithet. In 1956 and 1957, the board, for unspecified reasons, did not renew its contracts with two of the publishers, Giant Publishing and Globe Books, but retained a Harper & Brothers edition for use in high schools (ibid.). (The distance between the novel Twain wrote and the adaptations used by schools, including Scott, Foresman's and Globe's, is discussed in Ruth Stein, "The ABC's of Counterfeit Classics: Adapted, Bowdlerized, and Condensed," *English Journal* 55 [December 1966]: 1160–63).

6. Henry Louis Gates, Jr., *Loose Canons: Notes on the Culture Wars* (New York: Oxford University Press, 1992), 34.

7. Publisher's note, *Adventures of Huckleberry Finn*, ed. Emily Fanning Barry and Herbert B. Bruner (New York: Harper & Brothers, 1931), xi.

8. Barry and Bruner, introduction to *Adventures of Huckleberry Finn*, vii–viii. The editors were, in fact, so concerned about possible repercussions from the novel's former pariah status that they also asserted that *Huck Finn* "now stands proudly" on home library shelves (viii). Moreover, although the book on the home shelves was presumably the one Mark Twain wrote, the editors silently provided an expurgated edition.

9. Quoted in Nat Hentoff, *Free Speech for Me—But Not for Thee: How the American Left and Right Relentlessly Censor Each Other* (New York: HarperCollins, 1992), 21.

10. Louisa May Alcott, quoted ibid.

11. Since whites are implicitly considered the "norm" group, any group that deviates from this standard would be named. In this case, black children would have been identified as "negro," which was the editors' designation for Jim. (At that time, blacks' longstanding demand that the word be capitalized was widely ignored.)

12. Peaches Henry, "The Struggle for Tolerance: Race and Censorship in *Huckleberry Finn*," in *Satire or Evasion? Black Perspectives on "Huckleberry Finn,"* ed. James S. Leonard, Thomas A. Tenney, and Thadious M. Davis (Durham, N.C.: Duke University Press, 1992), 25.

13. See Jonathan Arac, *"Huckleberry Finn" as Idol and Target: The Functions of Criticism in Our Time* (Madison: University of Wisconsin Press, 1997), vii. (Arac also discusses hypercanonization at many other points in his book.)

14. Lionel Trilling, introduction to *Adventures of Huckleberry Finn* (1948), reprinted as "The Greatness of *Huckleberry Finn*" in *Adventures of Huckleberry Finn*, ed. Sculley Bradley et al., Norton Critical Edition, 2nd ed. (New York: Norton, 1977), 319.

15. T. S. Eliot, introduction to *Adventures of Huckleberry Finn* (1950), reprinted in *Adventures of Huckleberry Finn*, ed. Bradley et al., 328.

16. Trilling, "Greatness of *Huckleberry Finn*," 322.

17. Ibid., 324.

18. Albert E. Stone, Jr., *The Innocent Eye: Childhood in Mark Twain's Imagination* (New Haven: Yale University Press, 1961), 141–42.

19. Henry, "Struggle for Tolerance," 25.

20. "Huck Finn's Friend Jim," *New York Times,* September 13, 1957, p. 22.

21. Arac precedes us in noting that the editorial may implicitly suggest a connection between the suitability of Central High for teaching *Huck Finn* and the novel's treatment of Arkansas (see *Idol and Target,* 65).

22. Ibid., 10.

23. Joan DelFattore, *What Johnny Shouldn't Read: Textbook Censorship in America* (New Haven: Yale University Press, 1992), 132.

24. Donald B. Gibson, "Mark Twain's Jim in the Classroom," *English Journal* 57 (February 1968): 196 n. 1.

25. Edward Wagenknecht, *Mark Twain: The Man and His Work,* rev. ed. (Norman: University of Oklahoma Press, 1961), 222.

26. Andrew Solomon, "Jim and Huck: Magnificent Misfits," *Mark Twain Journal* 16 (Winter 1972): 20–21.

27. Laurence B. Holland, "A 'Raft of Trouble': Word and Deed in *Huckleberry Finn*," in *American Realism: New Essays,* ed. Eric J. Sundquist (Baltimore: Johns Hopkins University Press, 1982), 80.

28. DelFattore, *What Johnny Shouldn't Read,* 132.

29. Beverly P. Cole, "NAACP on *Huck Finn:* Train Teachers to Be Sensitive; Don't Censor . . . ," *Crisis* 82 (October 1982): 33.

30. DelFattore associates the council with the left-wing censor category, and then discusses the battle around *Huck Finn* without further mention of the council (*What Johnny Shouldn't Read,* 131–32).

31. *Publishers Directory,* 19th ed. (1998), lists the council and its address, but no phone or fax number. The council's articles on *Huckleberry Finn* were published in 1984 in its journal, *Interracial Books for Children Bulletin* (15, nos. 1–2, 4, 5). "Suggestions for Classroom Discussions of *Huck Finn*" appears in 15, nos. 1–2: 12. The last issue of the bulletin appeared in 1989.

32. See Hentoff, *Free Speech for Me,* 22.

33. John H. Wallace is the administrator who initiated an action to remove *Huck Finn* from the curriculum. His views, which have received extensive media attention, are discussed in chapter 10.

34. *Attacks on the Freedom to Learn: 1993–1994* (Washington, D.C.: People for the American Way, 1994), 195.

35. In 1998 the organization launched a statewide challenge to the novel as required reading. See Glenn Collins, "Twain Rolls on to New Heights: Film Rides a Wave of Interest in the Author," *New York Times,* July 15, 1998, E3.

36. Arac, *Idol and Target,* 11, 21.

37. Allen Carey-Webb, "Racism and *Huckleberry Finn:* Censorship, Dialogue, and Change," *English Journal* 82 (November 1993): 22. *Huckleberry Finn's* rank according to its use in public and parochial high school curricula is based on a 1989 survey, which also ranks the novel second only to Shakespeare in 56 percent of independent schools (see Arthur Applebee, "Stability and Change in the High-School Canon," *English Journal* 81 [September 1992]: 28).

38. Carey-Webb, "Racism and *Huckleberry Finn,*" 23–24.

39. Ralph Ellison, "Change the Joke and Slip the Yoke," *Partisan Review* 25 (Spring 1958): 222, 214–16.

40. James S. Leonard, "Blackface and White Inside," in *Satire or Evasion,* ed. Leonard, Tenney, and Davis, 122.

41. Richard White, quoted in Esther B. Fein, "Book Notes: Heathcliff and Huck Going Way of Scarlett," *New York Times,* February 5, 1992, C15. White is the author of *Mister Grey, or the Further Adventures of Huckleberry Finn* (New York: Four Walls Eight Windows, 1992).

42. Charles Miner Thompson, "Mark Twain as an Interpreter of American Character," *Atlantic Monthly,* April 1897, p. 446.

43. Bernard DeVoto, *Mark Twain's America* (1932; reprint, Westport, Conn.: Greenwood, 1978), 320.

44. Lauriat Lane, Jr., "Why *Huckleberry Finn* Is a Great World Novel," *College English* 17 (October 1955): 3.

45. Sherwood Cummings, *Mark Twain and Science: Adventures of a Mind* (Baton Rouge: Louisiana State University Press, 1988), 155.

46. William Dean Howells, quoted in Guy Cardwell, *The Man Who Was Mark Twain: Images and Ideologies* (New Haven: Yale University Press, 1991), 200. Howells made this statement in 1882, but Cardwell points out that he made comparable ones both earlier and later.

47. Louis J. Budd, "The Recomposition of *Adventures of Huckleberry Finn,*" Missouri Review 10 (1987): 113–29; reprinted in *The Critical Response to Mark Twain's "Huckleberry Finn,"* ed. Laurie Champion (New York: Greenwood, 1991), 196.

48. Henry Louis Gates, Jr., Introduction: "Writing 'Race' and the Difference It Makes," in *"Race," Writing, and Difference,* ed. Gates (Chicago: University of Chicago Press, 1986), 4, 5. For a multifaceted dissection of "race," see Ashley Montagu, *Man's Most Dangerous Myth: The Fallacy of Race,* 6th ed. (Walnut Creek, Calif.: AltaMira Press/Sage Publications, 1997).

49. Albert J. Raboteau, *A Fire in the Bones: Reflections on African-American Religious History* (Boston: Beacon, 1995), x.

Chapter 2: Marginal Boy

1. F. Scott Fitzgerald, quoted in Roy Harvey Pearce, "Yours Truly, Huck Finn," in *One Hundred Years of "Huckleberry Finn": The Boy, His Book, and American*

Culture, ed. Robert Sattelmeyer and J. Donald Crowley (Columbia: University of Missouri Press, 1985), 324.

2. Eliot, for instance, stated that Huck "sees the real world; and he does not judge it—he allows it to judge itself" (introduction, 329).

3. Trilling, "Greatness of *Huckleberry Finn*," 320.

4. Mark Twain, *The Adventures of Tom Sawyer* (New York: Vintage/Library of America, 1991), 45.

5. Ibid., 170.

6. The stricture against whites eating with blacks that began in the slavery era retained its potency for many decades thereafter. For instance, commenting on attitudes during the post-Reconstruction era, James M. McPherson states: "Next to interracial marriage, southern whites considered interracial dining the most heinous manifestation of social equality" (*The Abolitionist Legacy: From Reconstruction to the NAACP* [Princeton: Princeton University Press, 1975], 181).

7. *Tom Sawyer*, 212.

8. Ibid., 213.

9. Mark Twain, *Adventures of Huckleberry Finn*, ed. Walter Blair and Victor Fischer (Berkeley: University of California Press, 1988), chap. 4. All our quotations from *Huckleberry Finn* are from this edition, and will hereafter be cited parenthetically in the text.

10. Tom Quirk, *Coming to Grips with "Huckleberry Finn": Essays on a Book, a Boy, and a Man* (Columbia: University of Missouri Press, 1993), 94, 95.

11. Peter Messent, *New Readings of the American Novel: Narrative Theory and Its Application* (Houndmills, Basingstoke, Hampshire, England: MacMillan Education, 1990), 223.

12. Toni Morrison, *Playing in the Dark: Whiteness and the Literary Imagination* (Cambridge: Harvard University Press, 1992), 55.

13. Hortense J. Spillers, "Changing the Letter: The Yokes, the Jokes of Discourse, or Mrs. Stowe, Mr. Reed," in *Slavery and the Literary Imagination*, ed. Deborah E. McDowell and Arnold Rampersad (Baltimore: Johns Hopkins University Press, 1989), 28.

14. Henry Nash Smith, "A Sound Heart and a Deformed Conscience," in *Adventures of Huckleberry Finn*, ed. Bradley et al., 371.

Chapter 3: Shifting Perspectives

1. Alfred Kazin, afterword to *The Adventures of Tom Sawyer* (New York: Bantam Books, 1981), 221.

2. *Tom Sawyer*, 17.

3. Ibid.

4. Ibid.

5. Eric Lott points out that the song, as originally performed by blackface minstrels, was called "Lubly Fan" (1844) ("Mr. Clemens and Jim Crow: Twain,

Race, and Blackface," in *The Cambridge Companion to Mark Twain*, ed. Forrest G. Robinson [Cambridge: University of Cambridge Press, 1995], 132).

6. James B. Cade, quoted in Gladys-Marie Fry, *Night Riders in Black Folk History* (1975; reprint, Athens: University of Georgia Press, 1991), 97. Cade was a historian who, in 1929, undertook a study that recorded the testimony of ex-slaves.

7. Mary Kemp Davis, "The Veil Rent in Twain: Degradation and Revelation in *Adventures of Huckleberry Finn*," in *Satire or Evasion*, ed. Leonard, Tenney, and Davis, 77.

8. DeVoto, *Mark Twain's America*, 37, 76.

9. Chadwick Hansen, "The Character of Jim and the Ending of *Huckleberry Finn*," *Massachusetts Review* 5 (Autumn 1963): 46.

10. Fredrick Woodard and Donnarae MacCann, "*Huckleberry Finn* and the Traditions of Blackface Minstrelsy," *Interracial Books for Children Bulletin* 15, nos. 1–2 (1984): 5.

11. David L. Smith, "Huck, Jim, and American Racial Discourse," in *Black Writers on "Adventures of Huckleberry Finn" One Hundred Years Later*," ed. Thadious M. Davis, *Mark Twain Journal* 22 (Fall 1984): 4–12. Reprinted in *Satire or Evasion*, ed. Leonard, Tenney, and Davis, 108–10.

12. Forrest G. Robinson, "The Characterization of Jim in *Huckleberry Finn*," *Nineteenth-Century Literature* 43 (December 1988): 370–71.

13. A classic example of the use of the "ruined, for a servant" expression appears in a letter written in 1860 by the mayor of Savannah, Charles C. Jones, Jr., to his mother. Complaining of the influence of free black sailors on local slaves, Jones stated that they were "demoralizing our servants and ruining them in every point of view." The sailors were put under arrest, charged with "tampering with our Negroes" and "attempting to induce them to leave the state" ("Hon. Charles C. Jones, Jr., *to* Mrs. Mary Jones," in Robert Manson Myers, ed., *The Children of Pride: A True Story of Georgia and the Civil War* [1972], reprinted in 3 vols., vol. 2, *The Edge of the Sword [1860–1865]* [New York: Popular Library, 1972], 624).

14. Shelley Fisher Fishkin, *Was Huck Black? Mark Twain and African-American Voices* (New York: Oxford University Press, 1993), 83–84.

15. Fry states: "There is definitely a consensus of opinion among Blacks that whites dressed as ghosts. Texts of both the WPA Slave Narratives Collection, made in 1937, and the writer's own interviewing project, conducted in 1964 and 1972, agree completely on this point" (*Night Riders*, 79).

16. Ibid., 7, 79. Fry's point that the slaves could hold supernatural beliefs yet also recognize the fraudulence of the master's claims is illustrated by the recollections of Julia Henry, a former slave: "It was peoples made to pretend like they was ghosts. But they wasn't regular ghosts sure 'nough" (79).

17. Ibid., 74.

18. See Lorenzo J. Greene, Gary R. Kremer, Antonio F. Holland, *Missouri's Black Heritage*, rev. ed. (Columbia: University of Missouri Press, 1993), 38–39.

19. "Wasn't scared or superstitious," testified Jim Goff, a former slave in Texas. "One night old mistress hid in a corner of the fence to scare me. She put a sheet over her head and when I came by she jumped up to scare me. I didn't run. I just began throwing rocks and she ran out from there and didn't try to scare me again" (cited in Fry, *Night Riders*, 72).

20. Ibid., 93–95, 100–102. For an overall analysis of the patrol system, see 82–109.

21. Ibid., 6, 7. Fry's citation is from George Lyman Kittredge, *Witchcraft in Old and New England* (1929). According to Daniel G. Hoffman, Jim's witch beliefs are "without exception of European origin." He also notes that, with one exception (the hairball of an ox), all of Jim's other superstitions are also of European derivation ("Jim's Magic: Black or White?" *American Literature* 32 [March 1960]: 50, 52).

22. Robinson, "Characterization of Jim," 372.

23. Ibid., 371.

Chapter 4: Black Roots, White Roots

1. See Frances Trollope, *Domestic Manners of the Americans* (1832; reprint, ed. Donald Smalley, New York: Vintage, 1960), 221–22.

2. In castigating American slavery, certain European critics overlooked their own countries' involvement in the slave trade. Equiano, by contrast, was a British citizen whose autobiography was first published in London; it was addressed to "the English Parliament as part of a campaign to end the slave trade in the Empire," points out William L. Andrews (*To Tell a Free Story: The First Century of Afro-American Autobiography, 1760–1865* [Urbana: University of Illinois Press, 1986], 56). Although most of his personal experience as a slave was with a British master, Equiano was also enslaved for a short time on a Virginia plantation; later, as a free black seaman, he encountered injustices in such seaports as Charleston and Savannah (ibid.).

3. Ibid., 5.

4. Frances Smith Foster, *Witnessing Slavery: The Development of Ante-Bellum Slave Narratives*, 2nd ed. (Madison: University of Wisconsin Press, 1994), xxiii.

5. For a discussion of the authenticity of the slave narratives from a historian's standpoint, see John W. Blassingame, introduction to *Slave Testimony: Two Centuries of Letters, Speeches, Interviews, and Autobiographies*, ed. Blassingame (Baton Rouge: Louisiana State University Press, 1977), xvii–xlii. For analyses of the narratives' authenticity from the standpoint of literary critics, see Andrews, *To Tell a Free Story;* Foster, introduction and "'In Respect to Females . . .': Differences in the Portrayals of Women by Male and Female Narrators," *Witnessing*

Slavery; and Jean Fagan Yellin, preface and introduction to Harriet A. Jacobs, *Incidents in the Life of a Slave Girl: Written by Herself,* ed. Yellin (Cambridge: Harvard University Press, 1987).

6. Charles T. Davis and Henry Louis Gates, Jr., "Introduction: The Language of Slavery," in *The Slave's Narrative,* ed. Davis and Gates (Oxford: Oxford University Press, 1985), xviii.

7. Ibid., xii.

8. Ulrich B. Phillips, *American Negro Slavery: A Survey of the Supply, Employment, and Control of Negro Labor as Determined by the Plantation Regime* (1918; reprint, Baton Rouge: Louisiana State University Press, 1966), 291.

9. Kenneth M. Stampp, *The Peculiar Institution: Slavery in the Ante-Bellum South* (1956; reprint, New York: Vintage, 1989), 110–11.

10. Lewis Clarke, "Lewis Clarke: Leaves from a Slave's Journal of Life," in Blassingame, *Slave Testimony,* 153. Clarke's comments were made in a speech at an antislavery meeting, and recorded by Lydia Maria Childs; the speech was published in two parts in the *National Anti-Slavery Standard,* October 20, 27, 1842.

11. Gilbert Osofsky, "Introduction: The Significance of Slave Narratives," in *Puttin' On Ole Massa: The Slave Narratives of Henry Bibb, William Wells Brown, and Solomon Northup,* ed. Osofsky (New York: Harper & Row, 1969), 28.

12. John W. Blassingame, *The Slave Community: Plantation Life in the Antebellum South,* rev. ed. (New York: Oxford University Press, 1979), 200–201. Our comments on the slaves' escapes are based on Blassingame's account (ibid.) and Osofsky, *Puttin' On Ole Massa,* 28–30.

13. Fishkin, *Was Huck Black,* 107.

14. Lucinda H. MacKethan, "Huck Finn and the Slave Narratives: Lighting Out as Design," *Southern Review* 20 (April 1984): 255–56. William Wells Brown went on to write fifteen other books, including the first novel by an African American, *Clotel; or, The President's Daughter* (1853). In addition to being an exceptionally popular author, he was a prominent abolitionist; he was also involved in international reform movements, serving, for instance, as a delegate to the World Peace Congress in Paris in 1849 (see Henry Louis Gates, Jr., introduction to *Three Classic African-American Novels: Clotel; or, The President's Daughter,* by William Wells Brown; *Iola Leroy, or Shadows Uplifted,* by Frances E. W. Harper; and *The Marrow of Tradition,* by Charles W. Chesnutt; ed. Gates [New York: Vintage, 1990], ix–x).

15. The information on Brown and his mother is taken from William Wells Brown, *Narrative of William Wells Brown, a Fugitive Slave, Written by Himself* (1847), reprinted in Osofsky, *Puttin' On Ole Massa,* 204–10, 214–16.

16. Houston A. Baker, Jr., *Modernism and the Harlem Renaissance* (Chicago: University of Chicago Press, 1987), 17.

17. Mel Watkins, *On the Real Side: Laughing, Lying, and Signifying—the Under-*

ground Tradition of African-American Humor That Transformed American Culture from Slavery to Richard Pryor (New York: Simon & Schuster, 1994), 81.

18. Fishkin, *Was Huck Black*, 92.

19. Alexander Saxton, *The Rise and Fall of the White Republic: Class Politics and Mass Culture in Nineteenth-Century America* (London: Verso, 1990), 177, 176.

20. Robert C. Toll, *Blacking Up: The Minstrel Show in Nineteenth-Century America* (New York: Oxford University Press, 1974), 85. Before the mid-1850s, Toll states, minstrelsy displayed certain contradictory attitudes toward slavery, as revealed in its treatment of runaways: "To explain the fugitive's motivation, minstrels pointed to the injustices of bondage." On the other hand, "Minstrel ex-slaves either became pretentious dandies, incompetent fools, or joined the growing chorus of minstrel blacks who longed to return to their Southern homes, where they 'belonged.' For each unhappy slave they described, minstrels portrayed a number of happy ones. For every one that had to flee from a brutal master, minstrels described others who were given their freedom by benevolent masters. Some emancipated slaves refused to leave their idyllic plantation homes" (84, 85). Toll also declares: "From the outset, minstrelsy unequivocally branded Negroes as inferiors" (67).

Saxton writes: "Was minstrelsy monolithic in its justification of slavery? Almost, but not quite." There were, for instance, "a scattering of expressions" that entered minstrelsy through early borrowings from African-American culture that "carried anti-slavery connotations"; these, however, "might be negated in chorus or verses, perhaps added later" (*White Republic*, 176–77).

21. For instance, referring to the early minstrel shows, Twain wrote of "the real nigger show—the genuine nigger show, the extravagant nigger show—the show which to me had no peer and whose peer has not yet arrived. . . . We have the grand opera; and I have witnessed and greatly enjoyed the first act of everything which Wagner created. . . . But if I could have the nigger show back in its pristine purity and perfection I should have but little further use for opera" (*The Autobiography of Mark Twain*, ed. Charles Neider [New York: Harper & Row, 1959], 58–59).

22. Among the limited number of essentials required by slaves setting out on their journeys was a gun or a knife (see Blassingame, *Slave Community*, 200).

23. *Huckleberry Finn*, ed. Bradley et al., 40 n. 3.

24. An early criticism of Jim's failure to try for the Illinois shore was made by DeVoto, who contended that "there is a lordly disregard of the fact that Jim did not need to get to Cairo or the Ohio River, that he could have reached free soil by simply paddling to the Illinois shore from Jackson's Island" (*Mark Twain at Work* [Cambridge: Harvard University Press, 1942], 54). Answering this argument, Delancey Ferguson maintained that Jim could not have crossed over directly because he would have been quickly captured by slavehunters ("Clemens . . . *Huckleberry Finn*," *Explicator* 4 [April 1946]: item 42). While DeVoto over-

looked that slavehunters would likely be searching for Jim in Illinois, Ferguson overlooked that slavehunters do search for Jim on Jackson's Island.

25. *Huckleberry Finn,* ed. Bradley et al., 40 n. 3.

26. Fishkin, *Was Huck Black,* 107.

27. Stampp, *Peculiar Institution,* 120.

28. Robert Sattelmeyer, "Interesting, but Tough," in *One Hundred Years of "Huckleberry Finn,"* ed. Sattelmeyer and Crowley, 360. Sattelmeyer sees this incident as an inversion of the biblical episode in which Noah gets drunk on wine and lies uncovered in his tent. One of his sons, Ham, sees his father in this ignoble state and tells his two brothers. The brothers, without looking at their father, cover him up. Afterwards, Noah curses Ham, the presumed ancestor of African peoples, and prophesies slavery for his descendants. The incident was used in the antebellum South as "the principal justification for slavery." In Twain's version, it is not the son Huck "who covers his [father's] nakedness and shame," but the supposed descendant of Ham (ibid., 359–60). Sattelmeyer makes a persuasive case for the inverse analogy; however, since Twain replaced Noah's sons with Jim, there is no reason why he could not also have replaced the sons' motive with a different one for Jim.

29. Louis D. Rubin, Jr., *The Teller in the Tale* (Seattle: University of Washington Press, 1967), 65.

30. Jeffrey Steinbrink, "Who Wrote *Huckleberry Finn?* Mark Twain's Control of the Early Manuscript," in *One Hundred Years of "Huckleberry Finn,"* ed. Sattelmeyer and Crowley, 100. Steinbrink's use of "comfortable" comes from a remark Huck makes when he hears his father has drowned: "I warn't comfortable long," he says (chap. 3), after considering the evidence and deciding the dead person could not have been his father.

31. In his visit to the village, Huck learns from Judith Loftus that some people think Pap murdered Huck, while others think Jim did it. Commenting on the implications of the latter view, Robinson states that since "Huck is the living proof that Jim is not a murderer," he will provide Jim with "an alibi, and some small leverage when the inevitable disaster strikes" ("Characterization of Jim," 367). This would be a sound reason for Jim to keep Huck with him if disaster were in fact inevitable. But having escaped, Jim should act on the assumption that he can make his way to freedom, and decide on that basis whether Huck can help him. Robinson also sees Huck as giving Jim "eyes and ears, information" (ibid.); however, as we learn during the course of the voyage, Jim should not necessarily believe what Huck tells him.

Chapter 5: Shallows, Depths, and Crosscurrents

1. Robert Shulman, "Fathers, Brothers, and 'the Diseased': The Family, Individualism, and American Society in *Huck Finn,*" in *One Hundred Years of "Huckleberry Finn,"* ed. Sattelmeyer and Crowley, 336.

2. Lane, "Great World Novel," 5.

3. Michael J. Hoffman, "Huck's Ironic Circle," in *Mark Twain's "Adventures of Huckleberry Finn,"* ed. Harold Bloom (New York: Chelsea House, 1986), 38–39. In assigning symbolic meaning to Huck and Jim's nakedness, Hoffman, Lane, and Shulman seem also to be taking issue with Leslie Fiedler's view that the Huck-Jim relationship is implicitly homosexual. Fiedler's essay ("Come Back to the Raft Ag'in, Huck Honey!" *Partisan Review* 15 [June 1948]: 664–71) created shock when it was published. However, in 1995 Christopher Looby challenged Fiedler from a different perspective. Stating that his object was "to salvage from the essay what is genuinely useful," he stipulated that the "salvage operation requires that it initially be conceded that the essay does its thinking from within a deeply homophobic and gay-baiting structure of assumptions" ("'Innocent Homosexuality': The Fiedler Thesis in Retrospect," in *Mark Twain, "Adventures of Huckleberry Finn": A Case Study in Critical Controversy,* ed. Gerald Graff and James Phelan [Boston: St. Martin's, 1995], 535–36).

4. William Van O'Connor, "Why *Huckleberry Finn* Is Not the Great American Novel," *College English* 17 (October 1955): 6.

5. In 1956, Walter Blair answered O'Connor by stating that the downstream journey "give[s] the narrative coherence, allow[s] for a series of varied adventures and help[s] Twain say what he wants to say in the novel" ("Why Huck and Jim Went Downstream," *College English* 18 [November 1956]: 107). Henry Nash Smith concurred: "Why . . . did Mark Twain not cause Huck and Jim to make their way up the Ohio? To ask this question is to answer it: he did not know the Ohio. But he had known the lower Mississippi intimately" (introduction to *Adventures of Huckleberry Finn,* ed. Smith [Boston: Houghton Mifflin, 1958], viii).

6. Morrison, *Playing in the Dark,* 56.

7. This point is supported by the discovery, in 1990, of the first half of the manuscript of *Huckleberry Finn,* which had been presumed lost. The novel was composed in two stages, and it "had long been assumed that the first phase of composition" ended "where the riverboat runs over the raft. . . . Huck and Jim had passed Cairo in the fog, and the author was in the absurd position of having a runaway slave escaping into the deep South. . . . The evidence reveals, however, that Twain's first stint of composition got him well beyond this point," relates Quirk (*Coming to Grips,* 4–5).

8. Such preconceptions are reinforced by the illustrations of Jim in the original edition of *Huck Finn* (reprinted in at least two current editions). The illustrator Twain selected, E. W. Kemble, who made a career specialty of racist stereotypes, portrayed Jim as a "comic type bordering on caricature, his features and postures exaggerated, with the result that any distinct personality . . . [is] absorbed into what amounts to a racial abstraction," states Earl F. Briden ("Kemble's 'Specialty' and the Pictorial Countertext of *Huckleberry Finn,*" *Mark Twain Journal* 26 [Fall 1988]: 5).

9. Toll states: "When the endmen mocked [the interlocutor's] pomposity, audiences could indulge their anti-intellectualism and antielitism by laughing at him. But when he patiently corrected the ignorant comedians with their malaprop-laden dialects, audiences could feel superior to stupid 'niggers' and laugh with him" (*Blacking Up*, 53). Toll quotes T. Alston Brown, a theatrical manager, critic, and historian, who observed that the interlocutor is "always the same genial, gentlemanly, unruffled creature surveying the endmen . . . with the smiling forbearance which comes of innate superiority" (ibid.).

10. The contrast between minstrel humor and the slaves' own humor is illustrated by a slave tale that also involves stock. Where the joke in Jim's tale rests on his ignorance that "stock" has two meanings, the humor in the slaves' tale derives from their linguistic dexterity. In the tale—which was told by Josie Jordan, a former slave who heard it from her mother—a master is so stingy that his slaves' ribs "would kinda rustle against each other like corn stalks a-drying in the hot winds. But they gets even." On the day the hogs are to be killed, a field hand runs to the master: "The hogs is all died, now they won't be any meats for the winter." Taking a suffix denoting illness from a language acquired in an alien and hostile environment, the slaves create a mysterious disease that frightens the master:

> The master asks: "What's the illness with 'em?"
> "Malitis," they tells him, and they acts like they don't want to touch the hogs. . . .
> He says to keep all the meat for the slave families, but that's because he's afraid to eat it hisself account of the hog's got malitis.
> "Don't you all know what is malitis?" Mammy would ask the children. . . .
> "One of the strongest Negroes got up . . . long 'fore the rising horn called the slaves from their cabins. . . . When he tapped Mister Hog 'tween the eyes with [a heavy mallet], 'malitis' set in mighty quick." (Cited in Thomas L. Webber, *Deep Like the Rivers: Education in the Slave Quarter Community, 1831–1865* [New York: Norton, 1978], 98–99.)

11. Neil Schmitz, "The Paradox of Liberation in *Huckleberry Finn*," *Texas Studies in Literature and Language* 13 (Spring 1971): 132.

12. Lee Clark Mitchell, "'Nobody But Our Gang Warn't Around': The Authority of Language in *Huckleberry Finn*," in *New Essays on 'Adventures of Huckleberry Finn*,'" ed. Louis J. Budd (Cambridge: Cambridge University Press, 1985), 102.

13. David E. E. Sloane points out that Jim's notion of "many wives making life noisier than a boiler factory, with the boiler factory having the advantage of being able to shut down" can be traced to such literary comedians as Artemus Ward, who "used the same comic ideas in discussing Brigham Young and the

Mormons" (*"Adventures of Huckleberry Finn": American Comic Vision* [Boston: Twayne Publishers, 1988], 65).

14. Mary Boykin Chesnut, diarist and wife of a slaveowner, condemned the behavior of masters who maintained "harems," but simultaneously revealed her flagrantly white supremacist attitude toward black women by speaking of the "magnate who runs a hideous black harem with its consequences under the same roof with his lovely white wife, and his beautiful and accomplished daughters" (cited in Joel Williamson, *The Crucible of Race: Black-White Relations in the American South since Emancipation* [New York: Oxford University Press, 1984], 40).

15. Commenting on the masters' sales of their own children, Frederick Douglass stated, "Men do not love those who remind them of their sins . . . and the mulatto child's face is a standing accusation against him who is master and father to the child." And, too, there was the slaveowner's wife: "such a child is a constant offense to the wife. She hates its very presence, and when a slaveholding woman hates, she wants not means to give that hate telling effect"— means that included not only "kicks, cuffs, and stripes" but demands that their husbands sell these children (*My Bondage and My Freedom* [1855; reprint, ed. William L. Andrews, Urbana: University of Illinois Press, 1987], 42–43).

16. Woodard and MacCann, "Blackface Minstrelsy," 5.

17. Steven Mailloux, *Rhetorical Power* (Ithaca, N.Y.: Cornell University Press, 1989), 74.

18. Henry Louis Gates, Jr., *The Signifying Monkey: A Theory of African-American Literary Criticism* (New York: Oxford University Press, 1988), 4.

19. Douglass, *My Bondage and My Freedom*, 52–53. Among those African Americans who also recalled hearing African languages spoken was the physician, editor, writer, and abolitionist leader Martin Delany, whose Mandingo grandmother intoned chants about her homeland (see Ronald T. Takaki, *Violence in the Black Imagination: Essays and Documents*, expanded ed. [New York: Oxford University Press, 1993], 83). W. E. B. Du Bois recalled that the mother or wife of one of his eighteenth-century forebears was a Bantu, who "never became reconciled to this strange land," and sang a song from her homeland that "came down the years, and I heard it sung at my grandfather's fireside" (*The Autobiography of W. E. B. Du Bois: A Soliloquy on Viewing My Life from the Last Decade of Its First Century* [New York: International Publishers, 1968], 62). And the sociologist E. Franklin Frazier "claimed that he was of Ibo descent and he was very proud of it. He used to hear his grandmother use some Ibo words," recalled Marie Brown Frazier, his widow, in 1975 (quoted in Anthony M. Platt, *E. Franklin Frazier Reconsidered* [New Brunswick, N.J.: Rutgers University Press, 1991], 15–16). For a discussion of enslaved Africans' retention of their own languages, see Michael A. Gomez, *Exchanging Our Country Marks: The Transformation of African Identities in the Colonial and Antebellum South* (Chapel Hill: University of North Carolina Press, 1998), 173–82.

20. Arac takes note of Jim's remark and Missouri's French background, but does so to make a different point (see *Idol and Target*, 147).

21. Reports abound of the slaves' daring efforts to become literate. Douglass told of fellow slaves that he taught in his "Sabbath school": "These dear souls came not to Sabbath school because it was popular to do so, nor did I teach them because it was reputable to be thus engaged. Every moment they spent in that school, they were liable to be taken up, and given thirty-nine lashes. They came because they wished to learn. Their minds had been starved by their cruel masters" (*Narrative of the Life of Frederick Douglass, an American Slave, Written by Himself* [1845; reprint, New York: Anchor Books, 1973], 82–83). W. C. Nell, a black Garrisonian and historian, told of a talk he had with a female fugitive in Canada who had taught herself to read from books in her master's library. When she could not put them back without risking discovery, she burned them—evincing, as she described it, "a *burning desire* for knowledge" (cited in Osofsky, *Puttin' On Ole Massa*, 40).

Twain's notes show that he considered having Huck teach Jim to read: "Teaches Jim to read & write. . . . Had taught him a little before" ("Mark Twain's Working Notes," in *Adventures of Huckleberry Finn*, ed. Blair and Fischer, C-5, 753).

22. Robinson, "Characterization of Jim," 380.

23. Huck exhibits what Rhett S. Jones calls "white double-consciousness," a concept that adapts, or inverts, Du Bois's famous definition of black "double-consciousness" (see Jones, "Nigger and Knowledge: White Double-Consciousness," in *Black Writers on "Adventures of Huckleberry Finn" One Hundred Years Later*," ed. Thadious M. Davis, *Mark Twain Journal* 22 [Fall 1984]: 28–37. Reprinted in *Satire or Evasion*, ed. Leonard, Tenney, and Davis, 173–94).

Chapter 6: Identity Crisis

1. Stampp relates: "A slaveholder would abandon his lands and escape in the night with his movable chattels. The courts heard case after case like that of a Georgian who 'clandestinely removed his property, consisting of negroes, to . . . Alabama . . . to avoid the payment of his debts,' and of a Mississippian, who 'ran off . . . into Texas, certain negro slaves, with a view of defrauding his creditors.'" This story was repeated so often that "gone to Texas" was used to describe any debtor who ran off from his creditors (*Peculiar Institution*, 203).

2. MacKethan notes that Huck is "mouthing what must have been a common expression," but one that also relates to a scene in Douglass's *Narrative*. Douglass's mistress in Baltimore had begun to teach him to read until her husband found out and told her, "If you give a nigger an inch he will take an ell. . . . Now if you teach that nigger how to read, there would be no keeping him" ("Slave Narratives," 259).

3. Henry Nash Smith was the first to describe what Jim is up to: "The counterargument is provided by Jim, who seems to guess what is passing through Huck's mind, and does what he can to invoke the force of friendship and gratitude" ("Sound Heart," 370).

4. Pennington's account of his capture and escape appears in William L. Andrews, "Mark Twain and James W. C. Pennington: Huckleberry Finn's Smallpox Lie," *Studies in American Fiction* 9 (Spring 1981): 104–5.

5. Ibid., 107, 106.

6. Pennington, quoted ibid., 105.

7. We use "parent" because all Huck ever says about a mother who died early is that she and Pap fought (*Tom Sawyer*, 152).

8. Andrews, "Twain and Pennington," 103. MacKethan also points to parallels between *Huck Finn* and *The Fugitive Blacksmith*. For instance, when Jim believes he is near Cairo, his reaction ("Jump up and crack yo' heels") conforms to Pennington's description of himself when he reached free soil: "I ran, hopped, skipped, jumped, clapped my hands, and talked to myself" (quoted in MacKethan, "Slave Narratives," 260).

9. Commenting on the solidarity that existed among the slaves, George P. Rawick states, "The individual slave was never alone except when he ran away, and even then he often went from one community of slaves to the next, aided in his flight by his fellow slaves" (*From Sundown to Sunup: The Making of the Black Community*, vol. 1 of *The American Slave: A Composite Autobiography* [Westport, Conn.: Greenwood, 1972], 11). Despite reprisals from the master, it was usually futile for a master to expect help from other slaves in catching a runaway. "Even domestics often refused to be informers," states Stampp. "One house servant was whipped for not reporting that she had heard a runaway 'talking in the yard.'" Another owner demoted two house servants to field laborers for helping fugitives, and also tried to coerce his other slaves into informing (*Peculiar Institution*, 116).

10. Wendell Phillips, "Letter from Wendell Phillips, Esq.," in Douglass, *Narrative*, xxii.

11. Shulman, "Fathers, Brothers, and 'the Diseased,'" 336.

12. Just before the passage, in chapter 14, where they argue over French, Huck tells Jim a garbled story about Louis Charles, the son of Louis XVI, who was executed. According to legend, the young dauphin (who is believed to have died in prison) survived and escaped (see *Huck Finn*, ed. Bradley et al., 66 n. 7). Jim expresses naive concern for the poor little dauphin ("he'll be pooty lonesome—dey ain' no kings here, is dey Huck?" [chap. 14]). This tale presumably makes Huck and Jim receptive to the impostor's claim to be the dauphin (though one might think it would make them more wary).

13. "I used to try to learn the ways of these Negroes, but I could never divest myself of the suspicion that they were learning my ways faster than I was learn-

ing theirs," recalled Duncan Clinch Heyward, son of one of South Carolina's largest rice planters (quoted in Lawrence W. Levine, *Black Culture and Black Consciousness: Afro-American Folk Thought from Slavery to Freedom* [Oxford: Oxford University Press, 1977], 101). And a Virginia slaveowner concluded that blacks had their mental abilities "sharpened by constant exercise," and that their perceptions were "extremely fine and acute" (quoted in Stampp, *Peculiar Institution*, 87).

14. "A battery upon a white person might . . . carry a sentence of death under certain circumstances," states Stampp (*Peculiar Institution*, 210).

15. Rhett Jones observes: "When slave mothers wept as their children were sold away from them, the culture comforted white Americans by insisting that while the mothers seemed to be miserable, they were much like bitches deprived of their litter. The dog might miss them for a few days, but soon forgot her pups" ("Nigger and Knowledge," 178).

16. In a rare critique of Jim's treatment of his daughter, Ernest D. Mason states: "The simple truth is that Jim could have and perhaps should have closed the door himself; he had no right to 'fetch her a slap side de head dat sont her a-sprawlin' ' across the room. It is of little help, moreover, to interpret this scene as Jim's attempt to demand respect for his adulthood. On the contrary, what Jim does is enough to make Elizabeth lose respect for him altogether" ("Attraction and Repulsion: Huck Finn, 'Nigger' Jim, and Black Americans Revisited," *CLA Journal* 33 [September 1989]: 42).

17. Wilma King states: "Many slave parents demanded obedience from their children, but they were not sadistic. Their basic goal was to protect the children from harm at the hands of malicious whites" (*Stolen Childhood: Slave Youth in Nineteenth-Century America* [Bloomington: Indiana University Press, 1995], 69). Blassingame states: "Slave parents made every effort humanly possible to shield their children from abuse and teach them how to survive in bondage. One of the most important lessons for the child was learning to hold his tongue around white folks" (*Slave Community*, 186). A former slave, Elijah P. Marrs, said, "Mothers were necessarily compelled to be severe on their children to keep them from talking too much. Many a poor mother has been whipped nearly to death on account of their children telling white children things" (quoted ibid., 187). Some masters tried to get slave children to spy on their parents.

The enslaved mothers intervened at great risk to themselves to prevent their children from being abused by masters or overseers, while the children were instructed to protect their mothers. "W. H. Robinson was taught by his father that he should die, if need be, in defense of his mother" (Webber, *Deep Like the Rivers*, 172). Douglass tells of a woman who fought, unavailingly but valiantly, against an overseer who was trying to whip her—there was blood on his face as well as hers—while her children, aged about seven to ten, pelted him with stones; one seized the man's leg and bit him (*My Bondage and My Freedom*, 62–63).

18. Lott, "Mr. Clemens and Jim Crow," 140.

19. Davis, "Veil Rent in Twain," 83.

Chapter 7: Conscience Revisited

1. Williamson, *Crucible of Race*, 248–49.

2. See Gunnar Myrdal, *An American Dilemma: The Negro Problem and Modern Democracy*, vol. 1 (1944; reprint, New Brunswick, N.J.: Transaction Publishers, 1996), lxxix. Although abolitionists and civil rights advocates pointed to the conflict between white Americans' profession of democratic principles and their treatment of black Americans, Myrdal "did not merely argue that the contradiction existed; he insisted that white Americans experienced it as a mental conflict," states Walter A. Jackson (*Gunnar Myrdal and America's Conscience: Social Engineering and Racial Liberalism, 1938–1987* [Chapel Hill: University of North Carolina Press, 1990], xii).

3. David R. Roediger, *The Wages of Whiteness: Race and the Making of the American Working Class* (London: Verso, 1991), 133.

4. For an account of this conversion, see Noel Ignatiev, *How the Irish Became White* (New York: Routledge, 1995).

5. Arac takes issue with the view that Pap's character and flagrant racism typify the nineteenth-century portrayal of poor Southern whites: "as a type within the writing of Twain's time, pap is not a Southerner but a 'Pike,'" who shambles, drawls, drinks, and disrespects the rights of others (*Idol and Target*, 40). However, Hugh J. Dawson sees Pap as conforming to the Irish stereotype of the time, which presented Irish males as "dirty, lazy, drunken and violent" ("The Ethnicity of Huck Finn—and the Difference It Makes," *American Literary Realism, 1870–1910* 30 [Winter 1998]: 12). But the supposedly distinguishing traits of the Irish and Pike stereotypes also extend to "poor white trash" Southerners, thus illustrating the interchangeability of class and ethnic caricatures, which, as we have noted, can also be interchangeable with racial ones. (In certain respects, Pap, as a figure who is frightened as well as frightening, goes beyond stereotype.)

Arac also takes issue with the portrayal of Missouri in critical writings on *Huck Finn* as a "model for the 'South.'" Although a slave state and below the Mason-Dixon Line, it is not a Southern state; at the time Twain was born, it was the westernmost state: "At least two such opposed critics as Brooks and DeVoto agreed in understanding the dominant influence on the milieu of Twain's youth as the 'frontier'" (*Idol and Target*, 40, 41). But Missouri's status as a frontier state, important as this was, was eclipsed by its status as a slave state. Hannibal's population, Twain wrote, "had come from slave states and still had the institution of slavery with them in their new homes" (*Autobiography*, 28). This included Twain's own home, where slaves were owned, rented, and, particularly by his father but also by his mother, abused (see Arthur G. Petit, *Mark Twain and the South* [Lexington: University Press of Kentucky, 1974], 16–17).

6. Greene, Kremer, and Holland, *Missouri's Black Heritage*, 64.

7. Walter Blair believed that this represented Twain's own view, as illustrated by a fable he wrote. In 1875, the year before he started on *Huck Finn*, Twain sent the *Atlantic* a humorous sketch about a utopia that practiced universal (male) suffrage by giving "every citizen, however poor or ignorant," one vote, but adding additional votes as a man acquired more education or more property. Since education added more extra votes than did property, "educated men became a wholesome check upon wealthy men" (Twain, "The Curious Republic of Gondour," cited in Blair, *Mark Twain and Huck Finn* [Berkeley: University of California Press, 1960], 133–34). Interpreting the greater number of votes accorded for education as a check on wealth overlooks, among other things, the almost absolute correlation in the South of that time between race, socioeconomic status, and higher education.

8. By 1860, in the slave states as a whole, "mulattoes were a 400 percent higher proportion of the free black community than of the slave community," states James Oliver Horton (*Free People of Color: Inside the African American Community* [Washington, D.C.: Smithsonian Institution Press, 1993], 125). One significant reason why light-skinned slaves were freed at so disproportionate a rate is that their masters were also often their fathers.

9. Ibid., 139. Horton states: "The mulatto characteristics were generally attributed to the infusion of 'white blood.' This was seen as a dangerous combination that might explode in violence. Many whites would have agreed with one southern woman's belief that in the mulatto 'enough white blood [would] replace native humility and cowardice with Caucasian audacity'" (ibid.). The influence of the "black blood, white blood" thesis by no means disappeared with the nineteenth century. One of its frequent twentieth-century appearances is in a comment on *Huck Finn:* "[Twain] shows us the African in Jim, imbuing him with a dark knowledge that lies in his blood" (Gladys Carmen Bellamy, *Mark Twain as a Literary Artist* [Norman: University of Oklahoma Press, 1950], 340).

10. Lott precedes us in noting that Pap is in blackface when he delivers his monologue ("Mr. Clemens and Jim Crow," 130). However, Lott also interprets this scene as one that reflects "subterranean links between black and lower-class white men [that] called forth in the minstrel show, as in Mark Twain's work, interracial recognitions and identifications no less than the imperative to disavow them" (ibid.).

11. Charles C. Bolton states, "Slavery blocked the development of regular wage positions for white laborers; consequently, they moved frequently between

a wide variety of jobs, a life-style that allowed them to avoid starvation but offered few chances for economic advancement and independence. Likewise, white tenants could certainly make a living on their rented farms, but tenancy provided little . . . autonomy and security" (*Poor Whites of the Antebellum South: Tenants and Laborers in Central North Carolina and Northeast Mississippi* [Durham, N.C.: Duke University Press, 1994], 41).

12. Williamson, *Crucible of Race*, 18.

13. Sloane, *American Comic Vision*, 92, 97.

14. Philip S. Foner, *Mark Twain: Social Critic* (New York: International Publishers, 1958), 219.

15. Blair, *Mark Twain and Huck Finn*, 313–14.

16. Michael Egan, *Mark Twain's "Huckleberry Finn": Race, Class, and Society* (London: Published for Sussex University Press by Chatto & Windus, 1977), 132.

17. Clearly, this is Twain's means of expressing sympathy with the suffering of black women over lynching—they were not only its indirect but also its direct victims—in the post–Civil War era. But this touch, estimable in itself, is also consistent with his treatment of Jim, who—unlike the actual slaves, female as well as male—is a figure of suffering but not resistance (that is, one who abandons resistance). Black women's resistance to slavery was carried on in their post-slavery struggles against lynching (see, for instance, n. 20), as well as in many other ways.

18. Sherburn's murder of Boggs is based upon an incident that occurred in Hannibal, Missouri, in 1845. While drunk, Sam Smarr, a farmer, publicly accused William Owsley, a wealthy merchant, of cheating two of his friends. Two or three weeks later, Owsley came up behind Smarr, shouted out his name, and drew a pistol. Smarr begged Owsley not to shoot, but to no avail. Owsley was acquitted of the murder but, according to Twain, moved away because of the town's coldness toward him; however, Dixon Wecter cited advertisements showing that Owsley was still in business in Hannibal seven years after his acquittal (see Blair, *Mark Twain and Huck Finn*, 306–7, 313, 413 n. 4).

19. That one must be wary of analogies between lynchings of the frontier-justice type and white supremacist lynchings is also illustrated by the following: the implicit rationale for the attempted lynching in Bricksville, that the courts will not convict the guilty, had different connotations when applied to the lynchings of blacks in later eras. Such lynchings, it was alleged, were necessary because the courts would not convict blacks. Douglass answered: "The man in the South who says he is for Lynch Law because he honestly believes that the courts . . . are likely to be too merciful to the Negro . . . either does not know the South, or is fit for prison or an insane asylum" (Douglass, introduction to *The Reason Why the Colored American Is Not in the World's Columbian Exposition*, by Ida B. Wells-Barnett [1893]; reprinted in *Selected Works of Ida B. Wells-Barnett*, comp. Trudier Harris [New York: Oxford University Press, 1991], 57).

20. In the Reconstruction era, the Ku Klux Klan "was at first organized and headed by upper-class whites, and studied terror and violence were its chosen instruments" (Williamson, *Crucible of Race*, 295). W. J. Cash wrote that the "better men" of the South "let their own hate run, set themselves more or less deliberately to whipping up the hate of the common whites, and often themselves led these common whites into mob action against the Negro" (*The Mind of the South* [1941; reprint, New York: Vintage, 1991], 117). Ida B. Wells-Barnett, the crusader against lynching, personally experienced the phenomenon Cash describes: in 1892 she escaped being lynched only because the would-be perpetrators, leading citizens of Memphis, could not find her: "threats of lynching were freely indulged, not by the lawless element upon which the deviltry of the South is usually saddled—but by the leading business men" ("The Offense," in *Southern Horrors: Lynch Law in All Its Phases* [1892], reprinted in *Selected Works*, 18).

21. See Mark Twain, "The Suppressed Passages," ed. Willis Wager, in *Life on the Mississippi*, ed. Edward Wagenknecht (New York: Heritage Press, 1944), 412–16. The passage includes a reference to a then-current instance of frontier justice in Kentucky, as well as a generalized description of lynchings whose exact nature is hard to determine.

22. Twain, quoted in Justin Kaplan, *Mr. Clemens and Mark Twain: A Biography* (1966; reprint, New York: Touchstone/Simon & Schuster, 1983), 365.

23. While Twain suppressed his later writings on lynching, he published an editorial in the *Buffalo Express* in 1869 concerning a black man who was lynched and then declared innocent. Twain scathingly derided "those fine chivalric passions and that noble Southern spirit which will not brook the slow and cold formalities of regular law, when outraged white womanhood appeals for vengeance." However, at the same time that he appeared to unequivocally reject the rationale for lynching, he also said: "What if the blunder of lynching the wrong man does happen once in four or five cases?" Thus Twain's irony masked but did not hide an intimation that in most cases the lynched were guilty (see Twain, "Only a Nigger," reprinted in P. Foner, *Mark Twain*, 218).

The 1901 essay that Twain suppressed, "The United States of Lyncherdom," was published in 1923 (reprinted in *Mark Twain and the Three R's: Race, Religion, Revolution—and Related Matters*, ed. Maxwell Geismar [Indianapolis: Bobbs-Merrill, 1973], 33–40). Twain, who had lived in the North for decades at the time he wrote it, intended to publish the piece first in a periodical and then as the introduction to a history of lynching, until his trepidation caused him to relegate it to posthumous publication. However, as Woodard and MacCann note, "the essay's content, not Twain's timidity, is the important problem. . . . Twain condemns lynching primarily because it is not due process, but he ignores the principle of due process in his discussion of this particular case. His arguments are based upon an unsupported presumption of Black guilt." As Woodard and

MacCann also point out, Twain reiterates the myth of the black male as a threat to white womanhood ("Blackface Minstrelsy," 9–10). Twain's position on lynching was not peculiar to him, but accorded with that of the many white Northerners who, in Nina Silber's description, "condemned the final act of lynching" but "sympathized with the sentiments of protecting the sanctity of white womanhood" (*The Romance of Reunion: Northerners and the South, 1865–1900* [Chapel Hill: University of North Carolina Press, 1993], 154). Decades later, Cash would acknowledge that the chance of a white woman's being raped by a black man was "much less . . . than the chance that she would be struck by lightning" (*Mind of the South*, 115).

24. Twain, cited in DeVoto, *Mark Twain at Work*, 75.

25. Quirk, *Coming to Grips*, 66.

Chapter 8: Family Values

1. Trilling, "Greatness of *Huckleberry Finn*," 326.

2. For instance, in Blair's view, Huck's "making a moral decision" in this crisis and "then acting upon it show growing involvement and responsibility" (*Mark Twain and Huck Finn*, 332). Sloane maintains that "the most important . . . element in the Wilks sequence is the identification of a moral position for Huck. . . . He comes to a series of positions which establish the groundwork for his ultimate decision to save Jim" (*American Comic Vision*, 108). And Nancy Walker states that Mary Jane is "a significant influence on Huck's developing conscience." The passage describing his parting from her "marks the penultimate step in the moral development that culminates in his decision to risk his soul to help Jim" ("Reformers and Young Maidens: Women and Virtue in *Adventures of Huckleberry Finn*," in *One Hundred Years of "Huckleberry Finn*," ed. Sattelmeyer and Crowley, 184).

3. According to Twain, "To separate and sell the members of a slave family to different masters was a thing not well liked by the people [of Hannibal] and so it was not often done, except in the settling of estates" (*Autobiography*, 30). Thus, as is evident from Twain's remark, even if an owner preferred to keep a slave family together, his preference would, whenever deemed necessary, give way to financial considerations. These conflicting concerns are reflected in the notices slaveowners placed. For instance, one that appeared in the *St. Louis Republican* in 1849 offered a woman for sale on the condition that she was "not to leave the city." But the same notice offered a woman and her two children without stipulating that they be sold as a family; it also unconditionally offered an eleven-year-old girl (cited in Shelley Fisher Fishkin, *Lighting Out for the Territory: Reflections on Mark Twain and American Culture* [New York: Oxford University Press, 1997], 18).

4. Had Mary Jane located her slaves, she would have faced a long, arduous, and costly battle to get them back: "Slaveholders kept the courts busy with litigation involving titles and charges of fraudulent sales," points out Stampp (*Peculiar Institution*, 203). A legal battle to regain the Wilks slaves would have been particularly difficult (Mary Jane would have had to contend with two or three owners in different places), but there is little chance the matter would have reached the courts, given that the slavetraders undoubtedly supplied fake identities, a common practice. For instance, traders sometimes placed notices in which they described themselves as "planters" to create the impression that they wanted the slaves for their own use rather than for resale (see Frederic Bancroft, *Slave Trading in the Old South* [1931; reprint, Columbia: University of South Carolina Press, 1996], 36).

A vivid example of the deception involved in slave trading appears in a letter written in 1857 by a minister and slaveholder, Rev. C. C. Jones of Georgia, to his son: "Enclosed you will find a letter received today which will be as great a surprise to you . . . as it has been to us. The man Lilly who writes the letter is evidently a Negro trader, and not the permanent owner of the Negroes! The internal evidence of the letter proves it. . . . My opinion is that they are [in New Orleans] on sale! *Lilly* says *he bought them in Savannah*. This was not the *name* of the man who appeared in the purchase, nor was *New Orleans* his home. Was it not a *planter* near Macon who bought for his *own use* and not to sell again? Here seems to be deception—a wheel within a wheel!" ("Rev. C. C. Jones to Mr. Charles C. Jones, Jr.," in Myers, ed., *Children of Pride*, vol. 1, *Many Mansions [1854–1860]*, 309).

5. Rawick points out that escaped slaves who were captured sometimes committed suicide rather than go back to slavery (*From Sundown to Sunup*, 103). Stampp states that slaves "freshly imported from Africa and those sold away from friends and relatives were especially prone to suicide" (*Peculiar Institution*, 128). Vincent Harding recounts instances of this form of resistance on the slave ships (in one incident, a witness reported that he heard a "song of triumph" from the slaves who jumped overboard). "To call such acts 'passive resistance' is to deny the existence of vast realms of the spirit, to count resistance only by its outward physical modes." Although a "last resort," such acts "challenged and denied the ultimate authority of the white traders" over the lives and spirits of the blacks (*There Is a River: The Black Struggle for Freedom in America* [1981; reprint, San Diego: Harvest/Harcourt Brace, 1992], 18–20).

6. Twain was closely acquainted with the sale of slaves: his father, while on a trip to Tennessee in 1842, appears to have bartered one of his own. "Although the slave's fate is not certain, a promissory note given Judge Clemens . . . suggests that Charley was turned in for ten barrels of tar worth forty dollars," states Petit (*Mark Twain and the South*, 17). Twain, writing in 1890 or 1891, condemned

his father: Charley's "eternal exile from his home, & his mother, & his friends" was of no concern to Judge Clemens (cited ibid., 17–18). (Petit also notes that in *Huck Finn,* Jim is sold for "forty dirty dollars.") In 1823, the judge sold a seventeen-year-old youth to a man in Mississippi (ibid., 17).

7. Punishments for runaways included whipping, branding with a hot iron, and the wearing of balls, chains, and bells. Recaptured slaves also faced death: "At times slaves would be killed by masters in order to educate other slaves that captured runaways would not be let off with light punishments" (Rawick, *From Sundown to Sunup,* 59). Many fugitives were ready to fight to the death to prevent being captured: "Numbers of men who carried pistols and bowie knives vowed to kill anyone who tried to stop them. Some fought desperately for their lives when confronted" (Osofsky, *Puttin' On Ole Massa,* 29).

8. Arac dissents from the view that Huck's decision to go to hell is the outcome of a moral crisis. Referring to the incident in which Huck hears from Miss Watson about "the bad place" and wishes he were there, particularly after learning of her plans to go to the "good place," Arac states: "So from the beginning Huck has been ready to go to hell . . . there is therefore no actual drama to what is generally referred to as his 'crisis'" (*Idol and Target,* 34–35). In the opening pages, though, Huck is not seriously considering hell, he just wants to get away ("all I wanted was a change; I warn't particular"). In fact, he does not express a readiness to go to hell but to the "bad place," which, like all euphemisms, veils what it presumably stands for. The intimation that Huck does not actually contemplate hell at this point is reinforced when he asks Miss Watson if Tom Sawyer will go to the "good place," and is assured he will not. "I was glad about that, because I wanted him and me to be together" (chap. 1). It is extremely doubtful that Huck believes the respectable Tom would go to hell, which is surely populated by such demons as abolitionists.

9. During the time when Huck would have been making his decision, slaveowners became more systematic in suppressing antislavery opinion among whites. Around 1835, "vigilance committees" or "committees of safety" led by judges, militia officers, lawyers, merchants, and planters were formed. The committees meted out punishments ranging from those intended to humiliate (such as shaving the head, blacking the face, selling at public auction) to physical ones such as lashings, beatings, and stonings (see Russell B. Nye, *Fettered Freedom: Civil Liberties and the Slavery Controversy, 1830–1860* [East Lansing: Michigan State College Press, 1949], 142–52). In 1837, Missouri passed a law making it a felony to publish or promulgate abolitionist opinion. North Carolina had a death penalty for concealing a slave for the purpose of escape (Stampp, *Peculiar Institution,* 211). At least one prominent antislavery figure, the editor Elijah Lovejoy, was driven out of Missouri in 1836 by threats from proslavery forces; he was murdered later that year at the hands of an Illinois mob (for a biography of

Lovejoy, see Paul Simon, *Freedom's Champion: Elijah Lovejoy* [Carbondale: Southern Illinois University Press, 1994]).

Chapter 9: The Kindness of Friends

1. Thomas Sergeant Perry, review of *Adventures of Huckleberry Finn* (1885), reprinted in *Huck Finn among the Critics: A Centennial Selection,* ed. M. Thomas Inge (Frederick, Md.: University Publications of America, 1985), 34.

2. Ernest Hemingway, *Green Hills of Africa* (New York: Scribner, 1935), 22.

3. DeVoto, *Mark Twain at Work,* 92.

4. Trilling, "Greatness of *Huckleberry Finn,*" 326. Trilling defined "formal aptness" as a device that allows Huck to return to the anonymity he prefers (a curious desire in one who tells the tale of his own adventures), and Tom to assume the role of hero.

5. John Reichert, *Making Sense of Literature* (Chicago: University of Chicago Press, 1977), 197.

6. Leo Marx, "Mr. Eliot, Mr. Trilling, and *Huckleberry Finn,*" *American Scholar* 22 (Autumn 1953): 428, 427, 429–30.

7. Morrison, *Playing in the Dark,* 56.

8. E. L. Doctorow, [untitled], *New Yorker,* June 26/July 3, 1995, p. 132.

9. Morrison, *Playing in the Dark,* 57.

10. See James M. Cox, *Mark Twain: The Fate of Humor* (Princeton: Princeton University Press, 1966), 169–84.

11. George C. Carrington, Jr., *The Dramatic Unity of "Huckleberry Finn"* (Columbus: Ohio State University Press, 1976). Carrington's thesis also subsumes the ending-as-allegory view.

12. See Robinson, "Characterization of Jim," 388.

13. Eric J. Sundquist, *To Wake the Nations: Race in the Making of American Literature* (Cambridge: Harvard University Press, 1993), 232.

14. Lott, "Mr. Clemens and Jim Crow," 135.

15. Quoted in Harding, *There Is a River,* 99.

16. Harding states: "On one level, Turner was obviously living within the popular nineteenth-century Euro-American millenarian religious tradition, marked by a belief in the imminent return of Christ to rule his earth." Often, for "persons thus convinced, a terrible and sometimes beautiful urgency caught fire and burned within them." However, "the burning within Nat Turner came from an at once similar and very different fire" (ibid., 79–80). In 1831, Turner said: "I heard a loud voice in the heavens, and the Spirit instantly appeared to me and said . . . I should arise and prepare myself, and slay my enemies with their own weapons . . . for the time was fast approaching when the first should be last and the last should be first" (quoted ibid., 75).

17. Eric Foner, *Reconstruction: America's Unfinished Revolution, 1863–1877* (New York: Harper & Row, 1988), xix, xx. The citations are from Foner's summary of the views on Reconstruction of the historian William Dunning and his followers. Foner also states: "From the first appearance of the Dunning School, dissenting voices had been raised, initially by a handful of survivors of the Reconstruction era and the small fraternity of black historians." In 1935, Du Bois's *Black Reconstruction in America,* which presented a monumental challenge to the traditional interpretation of Reconstruction, "closed with an indictment of a profession whose writings had ignored the testimony of the principal actor in the drama of Reconstruction—the emancipated slave—and sacrificed scholarly objectivity on the altar of racial bias" (ibid., xxi).

18. See Harding, *There Is a River,* 97.

19. Although Cummings sees the ending as allegorical, he also states that "Twain took such pains to cover over [the allegory] that it is not likely to be seen by the casual reader" (*Mark Twain and Science,* 155).

20. E. Foner, *Reconstruction,* xxiv, xxvii.

21. See Eric Foner, "African Americans in Public Office during the Era of Reconstruction: A Profile," *Reconstruction* 2, no. 2 (1993): 20. Starting in 1865, a handful of blacks were given appointments, but black officeholding "began in earnest in 1867, when Congress, in the Reconstruction Act, ordered the election of new Southern governments," under suffrage rules that did not discriminate by race (ibid.).

22. Albion Tourgée, quoted in W. E. B. Du Bois, *Black Reconstruction in America, 1860–1880* (1935; reprint, Cleveland: Meridian/World Publishing, 1964), 621. Du Bois called Tourgée, who later became a well-known novelist, the "bravest of the carpetbaggers" (ibid.).

23. John Hope Franklin, *Reconstruction after the Civil War,* 2nd ed. (Chicago: University of Chicago Press, 1994), 154.

24. Rayford W. Logan names this number of terrorist groups whose activities accorded with the Klan's (*The Negro in American Life and Thought: The Nadir, 1877–1901* [New York: Dial Press, 1954], 10).

25. Franklin, *Reconstruction after the Civil War,* 203–4.

26. E. Foner, *Reconstruction,* 601.

27. Shapiro, *White Violence and Black Response,* 25.

28. Ibid., 23.

29. Ibid., 24–25.

30. William Ivy Hair, quoted ibid., 26.

31. Ibid.

32. Ibid., 26–27.

33. Plessy's associates in planning the action included P. B. S. Pinchback, the black former Reconstruction governor; Louis A. Martinet, a prominent black New Orleans physician and attorney; and the white Reconstruction judge

Tourgée. (For an account of the various stages of the battle around *Plessy v. Ferguson,* see Sundquist, *To Wake the Nations,* 233–47.)

Chapter 10: Fault Lines

1. President Bill Clinton, quoted in Kevin Sack, "In Little Rock, Clinton Warns of Racial Split," *New York Times,* September 26, 1997, A20; "Excerpts from President's Comments on School Desegregation," A20; the president's press secretary said the speech was "targeted at white America" (quoted in Sack, "In Little Rock," A1).

2. When she was a fifteen-year old student, Hazel Bryan Massery was captured in a famous photograph yelling "Go home nigger" at Elizabeth Eckford as she tried to enter Central High. Massery apologized to Eckford five years later. On the occasion of the fortieth anniversary, Massery said, "I grew up in a segregated society and I thought that was the way it was and that's the way it should be." Now she wants "to be the link between the past and the future. I don't want to pass this along to another generation" (quoted in Sack, "In Little Rock," A20).

3. State and local chapters of the NAACP stayed away from the event to protest a lack of progress in the area over the preceding forty years.

4. Hentoff, *Free Speech for Me,* 27.

5. This expression will be recognized as the ancestor of such contemporary ones as "I don't think of him/her as black" and "He/she transcends race."

6. Frederick Douglass, quoted in Jane H. Pease and William H. Pease, *They Who Would Be Free: Blacks' Search for Freedom, 1830–1861* (1974; reprint, Urbana: University of Illinois Press, 1990), 15.

7. Controversy in this respect has lately been revived around Harriet Beecher Stowe. For instance, in a defense of Stowe's opinions on race, Arac holds that from the 1920s into the 1940s, *Uncle Tom's Cabin* "suffered . . . from its association with progressive racial views" (*Idol and Target,* 98). But Stowe's views hardly qualify as progressive. They conform (as Arac acknowledges) to "romantic racialism" (see George Fredrickson, *The Black Image in the White Mind: The Debate on Afro-American Character and Destiny, 1817–1914* [1971; reprint, New York: Harper Torchbooks, 1972], 97–129). It is true, as Arac also states, that the "quite substantial differences" Stowe sees between the races are "not meant as pejorative" (*Idol and Target,* 94); however, her views on race cannot be judged merely at the level of intent, as illustrated, for instance, by the fact that she endowed Uncle Tom with the qualities—forbearance, piety, love of his masters, forgiveness of his torturer, and so forth—that she deemed exemplary in (dark-skinned) blacks. (Twain's portrayal of Jim also conforms to romantic racialism, albeit with certain contrarieties; e.g., while Uncle Tom can love even Simon Legree, Jim takes revenge on the king and the duke.)

Arac also states: "Although Tom's death comes through his nonviolent resistance, . . . he is nonetheless an activist (though since the 'New Negro' movement of the 1920s, many African Americans have devalued this personalistic, rather than political, mode of action)" (ibid., 102). While Arac dates African-American criticism of Uncle Tom from the 1920s, it began with the novel's publication. For instance, in a letter that appeared in *Frederick Douglass' Paper* in 1852, William G. Allen, a free black teacher, wrote: "Uncle Tom was a good old soul, thoroughly and perfectly pious. Indeed, if any man had too much piety, Uncle Tom was that man. . . . I believe . . . that it is not light the slaveholder wants, but *fire*, and he ought to have it. I do not advocate revenge, but simply, resistance to tyrants, if it need be, to the death" (cited in Richard Yarborough, "Strategies of Black Characterization in *Uncle Tom's Cabin* and the Early Afro-American Novel," in *New Essays on "Uncle Tom's Cabin,"* ed. Eric J. Sundquist [Cambridge: Cambridge University Press, 1986], 68–69). African-American writers, Yarborough indicates, will continue to strive to "distance themselves from all that *Uncle Tom's Cabin* represents" (ibid., 68).

(A full consideration of Arac's views on *Uncle Tom's Cabin,* including its historical role, is outside the concept and structure of our book, which was almost completed at the time his was published. However, such a discussion is particularly relevant because of recent suggestions that Stowe's novel either replace *Huck Finn* on the school curriculum [see Jane Smiley, "Say It Ain't So, Huck: Second Thoughts on Mark Twain's 'Masterpiece,'" *Harper's,* January 1996, p. 67] or join *Huck Finn* there [see Fishkin, *Lighting Out,* 196]).

8. The following illustrates why it is often so difficult to locate the author's voice in *Huck Finn:* in chapter 23, when Huck hears Jim mourning for his family, and finds it hard to believe that a black man could care for his family just as much as whites care for theirs, the distance between author's and narrator's voice is palpable—so much so that Lott refers to it as "one of Twain's heavier-handed interventions" ("Mr. Clemens and Jim Crow," 138).

Twain's attitude in this instance is presaged by a story he wrote shortly before he started work on *Huck Finn.* The nominal narrator, C—, asks his servant, a former slave, how she could have lived sixty years without ever having had any trouble. Despite her knowledge of whites, Aunt Rachel is shocked that C— could be so obtuse as to see nothing beyond her smiling mask: "Misto C—, is you in 'arnest?" After C—, fairly stammering in embarrassment, tries to explain away his denseness, Aunt Rachel tells how she, her husband, and her children were sold separately from each other. When the slavetraders are about to sell her last child, she threatens to kill any man who touches him. The men get the child away from her, but she tears their clothes and beats them over the head with her chain. They "give it to *me,* too, but I didn't mine dat" ("A True Story, Repeated Word for Word As I Heard It" [1874], reprinted in *The Complete Short Stories of Mark Twain,* ed. Charles Neider [New York: Bantam, 1958], 94–96).

On the question of blacks' love for their family, Twain's stance seems unequivocal, but in *Life on the Mississippi*, published shortly before *Huckleberry Finn*, he reverts to the attitude he derides in Huck. Writing of a black family pulling dogs aboard a steamboat, he remarks, "They must have their dogs; can't go without their dogs. . . . Sometimes a child is forgotten and left on the bank; but never a dog" (*Life on the Mississippi* [1883; reprint, ed. John Seelye, Oxford: Oxford University Press, 1990], 208).

9. Ellison, "Change the Joke," 215–16.

10. School official quoted in Hentoff, *Free Speech for Me*, 35. Hentoff states that the official requested anonymity.

11. W. E. B. Du Bois, "The Humor of Negroes," *Mark Twain Quarterly* 5 (Fall–Winter 1942–43): 12.

12. Quirk, *Coming to Grips*, 155.

13. Woodard and MacCann point out that a "serious problem" arises from "the fact that Jim refers to himself and other Blacks as 'niggers,' but the self-effacement inherent in his use of this term is not presented as a Black survival tactic. If Twain did not recognize the Black American use of such language as part of the 'mask' worn to disarm whites, he was, like Huck, caught unwittingly in the bigoted system that he could not always transcend. If he understood this strategy, but left out any hint of this awareness in order to please a white audience, then he compromised his literary integrity" ("Blackface Minstrelsy," 7).

14. The unidentified school official quoted in Hentoff, *Free Speech for Me*, 34.

15. Kay Puttock, "Historicism, *Huckleberry Finn*, and Howard Beach," *Teaching English in the Two-Year College* 17 (October 1990): 166–67.

16. John H. Wallace, "The Case against *Huck Finn*," in *Satire or Evasion*, ed. Leonard, Tenney, and Davis, 16. Wallace also has published an edition of *Huckleberry Finn* in which the racial epithet is removed. Although his edition, also bowdlerized in other ways, has often been denounced, the 1951 edition that also elides the epithet and bowdlerizes the novel in other ways has been criticized only rarely.

17. Tom Quirk, "Mark Twain," in *American Literary Scholarship: An Annual 1992*, ed. David J. Nordloh (Durham, N.C.: Duke University Press, 1994), 87.

18. Wallace, quoted in Hentoff, *Free Speech for Me*, 24.

19. Allen B. Ballard, [untitled], *Interracial Books for Children Bulletin* 15, nos. 1–2 (1984): 11.

20. Sonia Sanchez, [untitled], ibid.

21. Darryl Pinckney, *High Cotton* (1992; reprint, New York: Penguin, 1993), 109. The novel won the *Los Angeles Times* Book Prize for Fiction.

22. Toni Morrison, introduction to *Adventures of Huckleberry Finn* (New York: Oxford University Press, 1996), xxxi.

23. Ibid., xxxi–xxxii.

24. Margot Allen, "*Huck Finn:* Two Generations of Pain," *Interracial Books for Children Bulletin* 15, no. 5 (1984): 9.

25. Ibid., 9–12.

26. Julius Lester, "Morality and *Adventures of Huckleberry Finn,*" in *Satire or Evasion,* ed. Leonard, Tenney, and Davis, 200.

27. Morrison, introduction, xli.

28. Stephen Railton, "Jim and Mark Twain: What Do Dey Stan' For?" *Virginia Quarterly Review* 63 (Summer 1987): 393.

29. Puttock, "Historicism, *Huckleberry Finn,* and Howard Beach," 165.

30. Marylee Hengstebeck, "*Huck Finn,* Slavery, and Me," *English Journal* 82 (November 1993): 32. Carey-Webb was told by a black college student that "while a black teacher might be able to read *Huckleberry Finn* aloud, a white teacher, no matter how 'sympathetic,' simply could not without offending black students" ("Racism and *Huckleberry Finn,*" 28).

31. Wayne C. Booth, *The Company We Keep: An Ethics of Fiction* (Berkeley: University of California Press, 1988), 3–4.

32. Arac, *Idol and Target,* 14, 206.

33. Quirk, "Mark Twain," 87.

34. Leo Marx, "Huck at 100," in *Critical Response to Mark Twain's "Huckleberry Finn,"* ed. Champion, 165. According to the Office for Intellectual Freedom of the American Library Association, except in one case, all protests over *Huck Finn* between 1976 and 1984 involved one request: that the novel be discontinued as required reading. The exception—when parents also asked that the novel be removed from school libraries—occurred when a black child was abused by other students after his class read *Huck Finn* (see "On *Huck,* Criticism, and Censorship," *Interracial Books for Children Bulletin* 15, nos. 1–2 [1984]: 3). (The incident in question is discussed later in this chapter.)

35. Marx, "Huck at 100," 167.

36. Carey-Webb, "Racism and *Huckleberry Finn,*" 33, 23.

37. Hentoff, *Free Speech for Me,* 28. Although Hentoff discounts the charge of physical abuse (without verifying the matter one way or the other), he acknowledges the "constant taunting" of the boy as a "nigger" (26–27). Initially, black parents urged that the novel be removed from junior high school reading lists and school libraries. The compromise, which kept it in the libraries and gave district teachers the option of teaching it in the tenth grade, pleased both the parents and school officials, reports Hentoff—who was not pleased. Commenting on Hentoff's reaction, Peaches Henry states that he "mockingly reports the compromise agreed upon by parents and school officials, declaring it a 'victory for niceness'" ("Struggle for Tolerance," 30). (Hentoff originally reported on this incident, which occurred in Warrington, Pennsylvania, in a May 18, 1982, *Village Voice* article.)

38. Puttock, "Historicism, *Huckleberry Finn,* and Howard Beach," 167.

39. Booth, *Company We Keep,* 477–78.

Afterword

1. Lee Sigelman and Susan Welch, *Black Americans' Views of Racial Inequality: The Dream Deferred* (Cambridge: University of Cambridge Press, 1991), 1, 3. So far as the authors know, the first major survey to include blacks' opinions was not published until 1966; it dealt with the South. A national survey of black opinion was published two years later, followed by a fifteen-year hiatus before the next (ibid., 2).

Works Cited

Allen, Margot. "*Huck Finn:* Two Generations of Pain." *Interracial Books for Children Bulletin* 15, no. 5 (1984): 9–12.

Andrews, William L. "Mark Twain and James W. C. Pennington: Huckleberry Finn's Smallpox Lie." *Studies in American Fiction* 9 (Spring 1981): 103–12.

———. *To Tell a Free Story: The First Century of Afro-American Autobiography, 1760–1865.* Urbana: University of Illinois Press, 1986.

Applebee, Arthur N. "Stability and Change in the High-School Canon." *English Journal* 81 (September 1992): 27–32.

Arac, Jonathan. *"Huckleberry Finn" as Idol and Target: The Functions of Criticism in Our Time.* Madison: University of Wisconsin Press, 1997.

Attacks on the Freedom to Learn, 1993–1994. Washington, D.C.: People for the American Way, 1994.

Baker, Houston A., Jr. *Modernism and the Harlem Renaissance.* Chicago: University of Chicago Press, 1987.

Ballard, Allen B. [Untitled]. *Interracial Books for Children Bulletin* 15, nos. 1–2 (1984): 11.

Bancroft, Frederic. *Slave Trading in the Old South.* 1931. Reprint, Columbia: University of South Carolina Press, 1996.

Barry, Emily Fanning, and Herbert B. Bruner, eds. *The Adventures of Huckleberry Finn.* New York: Harper & Brothers, 1931.

Bellamy, Gladys Carmen. *Mark Twain as a Literary Artist.* Norman: University of Oklahoma Press, 1950.

Blair, Walter. *Mark Twain and Huck Finn.* Berkeley: University of California Press, 1960.

———. "Why Huck and Jim Went Downstream." *College English* 18 (November 1956): 106–7.

Blassingame, John W. *The Slave Community: Plantation Life in the Antebellum South.* Rev. ed. New York: Oxford University Press, 1979.

———, ed. *Slave Testimony: Two Centuries of Letters, Speeches, Interviews, and Autobiographies.* Baton Rouge: Louisiana State University Press, 1977.

Bolton, Charles C. *Poor Whites of the Antebellum South: Tenants and Laborers in Central North Carolina and Northeast Mississippi.* Durham, N.C.: Duke University Press, 1994.

Booth, Wayne C. *The Company We Keep: An Ethics of Fiction.* Berkeley: University of California Press, 1988.

Bradley, Sculley, et al., eds. *Adventures of Huckleberry Finn.* Norton Critical Edition. 2nd ed. New York: Norton, 1977.

Briden, Earl F. "Kemble's 'Specialty' and the Pictorial Countertext of *Huckleberry Finn.*" *Mark Twain Journal* 26 (Fall 1988): 2–14.

Brown, William Wells. *Narrative of William Wells Brown, a Fugitive Slave, Written by Himself.* 1847. Reprinted in *Puttin' on Ole Massa,* ed. Gilbert Osofsky. New York: Harper & Row, 1969.

Budd, Louis J. "The Recomposition of *Adventures of Huckleberry Finn.*" *Missouri Review* 10 (1987): 113–29. Reprinted in *The Critical Response to Mark Twain's "Huckleberry Finn,"* ed. Laurie Champion. New York: Greenwood, 1991.

Buder, Leonard. "*Huck Finn* Barred as Textbook by City." *New York Times,* September 12, 1957, pp. 1, 29.

Burke, Kenneth. *The Philosophy of Literary Form: Studies in Symbolic Action.* Baton Rouge: Louisiana State University Press, 1941.

Cardwell, Guy. *The Man Who Was Mark Twain: Images and Ideologies.* New Haven: Yale University Press, 1991.

Carey-Webb, Allen. "Racism and *Huckleberry Finn:* Censorship, Dialogue, and Change." *English Journal* 82 (November 1993): 22–34.

Carrington, George C., Jr. *The Dramatic Unity of "Huckleberry Finn."* Columbus: Ohio State University Press, 1976.

Cash, W. J. *The Mind of the South.* 1941. Reprint, New York: Vintage, 1991.

Champion, Laurie, ed. *The Critical Response to Mark Twain's "Huckleberry Finn."* New York: Greenwood, 1991.

Clarke, Lewis. "Lewis Clarke: Leaves from a Slave's Journal of Life." 1842. Reprinted in *Slave Testimony: Two Centuries of Letters, Speeches, Interviews, and Autobiographies,* ed. John W. Blassingame. Baton Rouge: Louisiana State University Press, 1977.

Cole, Beverly P. "NAACP on *Huck Finn:* Train Teachers to Be Sensitive; Don't Censor . . . " *Crisis* 82 (October 1982): 33.

Collins, Glenn. "Twain Rolls on to New Heights: Film Rides a Wave of Interest in the Author." *New York Times,* July 15, 1998, E3.

Cox, James M. *Mark Twain: The Fate of Humor.* Princeton: Princeton University Press, 1966.

Cummings, Sherwood. *Mark Twain and Science: Adventures of a Mind.* Baton Rouge: Louisiana State University Press, 1988.

Davis, Charles T., and Henry Louis Gates, Jr., eds. *The Slave's Narrative.* Oxford: Oxford University Press, 1985.

Davis, Mary Kemp. "The Veil Rent in Twain: Degradation and Revelation in *Adventures of Huckleberry Finn.*" In *Satire or Evasion? Black Perspectives on "Huckleberry Finn,"* ed. James S. Leonard, Thomas A. Tenney, and Thadious M. Davis. Durham, N.C.: Duke University Press, 1992.

Dawson, Hugh J. "The Ethnicity of Huck Finn—and the Difference It Makes." *American Literary Realism, 1870–1910* 30 (Winter 1998): 1–16.

DelFattore, Joan. *What Johnny Shouldn't Read: Textbook Censorship in America.* New Haven: Yale University Press, 1992.

DeVoto, Bernard. *Mark Twain at Work.* Cambridge: Harvard University Press, 1942.

———. *Mark Twain's America.* 1932. Reprint, Westport, Conn.: Greenwood, 1978.

Doctorow, E. L. [Untitled]. *New Yorker,* June 26/July 3, 1995, p. 132.

Douglass, Frederick. Introduction to *The Reason Why the Colored American Is Not in the World's Columbian Exposition,* by Ida B. Wells-Barnett. 1893. Reprinted in *Selected Works of Ida B. Wells-Barnett,* comp. Trudier Harris. New York: Oxford University Press, 1991.

———. *My Bondage and My Freedom.* 1855. Reprint, ed. William L. Andrews, Urbana: University of Illinois Press, 1987.

———. *Narrative of the Life of Frederick Douglass, an American Slave. Written by Himself.* 1845. Reprint, New York: Anchor Books, 1973.

Du Bois, W. E. B. *The Autobiography of W. E. B. Du Bois: A Soliloquy on Viewing My Life from the Last Decade of Its First Century.* New York: International Publishers, 1968.

———. *Black Reconstruction in America, 1860–1880.* 1935. Reprint, Cleveland: Meridian/World Publishing, 1964.

———. "The Humor of Negroes." *Mark Twain Quarterly* 5 (Fall–Winter 1942–43): 12.

Egan, Michael. *Mark Twain's "Huckleberry Finn": Race, Class, and Society.* London: Published for Sussex University Press by Chatto & Windus, 1977.

Eliot, T. S. From introduction to *Adventures of Huckleberry Finn.* 1950. Reprinted in *Adventures of Huckleberry Finn,* ed. Sculley Bradley et al. Norton Critical Edition. 2nd ed. New York: Norton, 1977.

Ellison, Ralph. "Change the Joke and Slip the Yoke." *Partisan Review* 25 (Spring 1958): 212–22.

Fein, Esther B. "Book Notes: Heathcliff and Huck Going Way of Scarlett." *New York Times,* February 5, 1992, C15.

Ferguson, Delancey. "Clemens . . . *Huckleberry Finn.*" *Explicator* 4 (April 1946): item 42.

Fiedler, Leslie. "Come Back to the Raft Ag'in, Huck Honey!" *Partisan Review* 15 (June 1948): 664–71.

Fishkin, Shelley Fisher. *Lighting Out for the Territory: Reflections on Mark Twain and American Culture.* New York: Oxford University Press, 1997.

———. *Was Huck Black? Mark Twain and African-American Voices.* New York: Oxford University Press, 1993.

Foner, Eric. "African Americans in Public Office during the Era of Reconstruction: A Profile." *Reconstruction* 2, no. 2 (1993): 20–32.

———. *Reconstruction: America's Unfinished Revolution, 1863–1877.* New York: Harper & Row, 1988.

Foner, Philip. *Mark Twain: Social Critic.* New York: International Publishers, 1958.

Foster, Frances Smith. *Witnessing Slavery: The Development of Ante-Bellum Slave Narratives.* 2nd ed. Madison: University of Wisconsin Press, 1994.

Franklin, John Hope. *Reconstruction after the Civil War.* 2nd ed. Chicago: University of Chicago Press, 1994.

Fredrickson, George. *The Black Image in the White Mind: The Debate on Afro-American Character and Destiny, 1817–1914.* 1971. Reprint, New York: Harper Torchbooks, 1972.

Fry, Gladys-Marie. *Night Riders in Black Folk History.* 1975. Reprint, Athens: University of Georgia Press, 1991.

Gates, Henry Louis, Jr. Introduction: "Writing 'Race' and the Difference It Makes." In *"Race," Writing, and Difference,* ed. Gates. Chicago: University of Chicago Press, 1985.

———. *Loose Canons: Notes on the Culture Wars.* New York: Oxford University Press, 1992.

———. *The Signifying Monkey: A Theory of African-American Literary Criticism.* New York: Oxford University Press, 1988.

———, ed. *Three Classic African-American Novels: Clotel; or, the President's Daughter,* by William Wells Brown; *Iola Leroy,* by Frances E. W. Harper; and *The Marrow of Tradition,* by Charles W. Chesnutt. New York: Vintage, 1990.

Gibson, Donald B. "Mark Twain's Jim in the Classroom." *English Journal* 57 (February 1968): 196–99, 202.

Gomez, Michael A. *Exchanging Our Country Marks: The Transformation of African Identities in the Colonial and Antebellum South.* Chapel Hill: University of North Carolina Press, 1998.

Greene, Lorenzo J., Gary R. Kremer, and Antonio F. Holland. *Missouri's Black Heritage.* Rev. ed. Columbia: University of Missouri Press, 1993.

Hansen, Chadwick. "The Character of Jim and the Ending of *Huckleberry Finn*." *Massachusetts Review* 5 (Autumn 1963): 45–66.

Harding, Vincent. *There Is a River: The Black Struggle for Freedom in America*. 1981. Reprint, San Diego: Harvest/Harcourt Brace, 1992.

Hemingway, Ernest. *Green Hills of Africa*. New York: Scribner, 1935.

Hengstebeck, Marylee. "*Huck Finn*, Slavery, and Me." *English Journal* 82 (November 1993): 32.

Henry, Peaches. "The Struggle for Tolerance: Race and Censorship in *Huckleberry Finn*." In *Satire or Evasion? Black Perspectives on "Huckleberry Finn,"* ed. James S. Leonard, Thomas A. Tenney, and Thadious M. Davis. Durham, N.C.: Duke University Press, 1992.

Hentoff, Nat. *Free Speech for Me—But Not for Thee: How the American Left and Right Relentlessly Censor Each Other*. New York: HarperCollins, 1992.

Hoffman, Daniel G. "Jim's Magic: Black or White?" *American Literature* 32 (March 1960): 47–54.

Hoffman, Michael J. "Huck's Ironic Circle." In *Mark Twain's "Adventures of Huckleberry Finn,"* ed. Harold Bloom. New York: Chelsea House, 1986.

Holland, Laurence B. "A 'Raft of Trouble': Word and Deed in *Huckleberry Finn*." In *American Realism: New Essays,* ed. Eric J. Sundquist. Baltimore: Johns Hopkins University Press, 1982.

Horton, James Oliver. *Free People of Color: Inside the African American Community*. Washington: Smithsonian Institution Press, 1993.

"Huck Finn's Friend Jim." *New York Times,* September 13, 1957, p. 22.

Ignatiev, Noel. *How the Irish Became White*. New York: Routledge, 1995.

Jackson, Walter A. *Gunnar Myrdal and America's Conscience: Social Engineering and Racial Liberalism, 1938–1987*. Chapel Hill: University of North Carolina Press, 1990.

Jones, Rhett S. "Nigger and Knowledge: White Double-Consciousness in *Adventures of Huckleberry Finn*." In *Black Writers on "Adventures of Huckleberry Finn" One Hundred Years Later,* ed. Thadious M. Davis. *Mark Twain Journal* 22 (Fall 1984): 28–37. Reprinted in *Satire or Evasion? Black Perspectives on "Huckleberry Finn,"* ed. James S. Leonard, Thomas A. Tenney, and Thadious M. Davis. Durham, N.C.: Duke University Press, 1992.

Kaplan, Justin. *Mr. Clemens and Mark Twain: A Biography*. 1966. Reprint, New York: Touchstone/Simon & Schuster, 1983.

Kazin, Alfred. Afterword to *The Adventures of Tom Sawyer*. New York: Bantam, 1981.

King, Wilma. *Stolen Childhood: Slave Youth in Nineteenth-Century America*. Bloomington: Indiana University Press, 1995.

Lane, Lauriat, Jr. "Why *Huckleberry Finn* Is a Great World Novel." *College English* 17 (October 1955): 1–5.

Leonard, James S. "Blackface and White Inside." In *Satire or Evasion? Black Perspectives on "Huckleberry Finn,"* ed. Leonard, Thomas A. Tenney, and Thadious M. Davis. Durham, N.C.: Duke University Press, 1992.

Leonard, James S., Thomas A. Tenney, and Thadious M. Davis, eds. *Satire or Evasion? Black Perspectives on "Huckleberry Finn."* Durham, N.C.: Duke University Press, 1992.

Lester, Julius. "Morality and Adventures of *Huckleberry Finn.*" In *Black Writers on "Adventures of Huckleberry Finn" One Hundred Years Later,* ed. Thadious M. Davis. *Mark Twain Journal* 22 (Fall 1984): 43–46. Reprinted in *Satire or Evasion? Black Perspectives on "Huckleberry Finn,"* ed. James S. Leonard, Thomas A. Tenney, and Thadious M. Davis. Durham, N.C.: Duke University Press, 1992.

Levine, Lawrence W. *Black Culture and Black Consciousness: Afro-American Folk Thought from Slavery to Freedom.* Oxford: Oxford University Press, 1977.

Logan, Rayford W. *The Negro in American Life and Thought: The Nadir, 1877–1901.* New York: Dial Press, 1954.

Looby, Christopher. "'Innocent Homosexuality': The Fiedler Thesis in Retrospect." In *Mark Twain, "Adventures of Huckleberry Finn": A Case Study in Critical Controversy,* ed. Gerald Graff and James Phelan. Boston: St. Martin's, 1995.

Lott, Eric. "Mr. Clemens and Jim Crow: Twain, Race, and Blackface." In *The Cambridge Companion to Mark Twain,* ed. Forrest G. Robinson. Cambridge: University of Cambridge Press, 1995.

MacKethan, Lucinda H. "Huck Finn and the Slave Narratives: Lighting Out as Design." *Southern Review* 20 (April 1984): 247–64.

Mailloux, Steven. *Rhetorical Power.* Ithaca, N.Y.: Cornell University Press, 1989.

Marx, Leo. "Huck at 100." *Nation,* August 31, 1985, pp. 150–52. Reprinted in *The Critical Response to Mark Twain's "Huckleberry Finn,"* ed. Laurie Champion. New York: Greenwood, 1991.

———. "Mr. Eliot, Mr. Trilling, and *Huckleberry Finn.*" *American Scholar* 22 (Autumn 1953): 423–40.

Mason, Ernest D. "Attraction and Repulsion: Huck Finn, 'Nigger' Jim, and Black Americans Revisited." *CLA Journal* 33 (September 1989): 36–48.

McPherson, James M. *The Abolitionist Legacy: From Reconstruction to the NAACP.* Princeton: Princeton University Press, 1975.

Messent, Peter. *New Readings of the American Novel: Narrative Theory and Its Application.* Houndmills, Basingstoke, Hampshire, England: MacMillan Education, 1990.

Mitchell, Lee Clark. "'Nobody But Our Gang Warn't Around': The Authority of Language in *Huckleberry Finn.*" In *New Essays on "Adventures of Huckleberry Finn,"* ed. Louis J. Budd. Cambridge: Cambridge University Press, 1985.

Montagu, Ashley. *Man's Most Dangerous Myth: The Fallacy of Race.* 6th ed. Walnut Creek, Calif.: AltaMira Press/Sage Publications, 1997.

Morrison, Toni. Introduction to *Adventures of Huckleberry Finn.* New York: Oxford University Press, 1996.

———. *Playing in the Dark: Whiteness and the Literary Imagination.* Cambridge: Harvard University Press, 1992.

Myers, Robert Manson, ed. *The Children of Pride: A True Story of Georgia and the Civil War.* 1972. Reprinted in 3 vols. *Many Mansions (1854–1860),* vol. 1; *The Edge of the Sword (1860–1865),* vol. 2. New York: Popular Library, 1972.

Myrdal, Gunnar. *An American Dilemma: The Negro Problem and Modern Democracy.* 2 vols. 1944. Reprint, New Brunswick, N.J.: Transaction Publishers, 1996.

Nye, Russell B. *Fettered Freedom: Civil Liberties and the Slavery Controversy, 1830–1860.* East Lansing: Michigan State College Press, 1949.

O'Connor, William Van. "Why *Huckleberry Finn* Is Not the Great American Novel." *College English* 17 (October 1955): 6–10.

"On Huck, Criticism, and Censorship." *Interracial Books for Children Bulletin* 15, nos. 1–2 (1984): 3.

Osofsky, Gilbert, ed. *Puttin' On Ole Massa: The Slave Narratives of Henry Bibb, William Wells Brown, and Solomon Northup.* New York: Harper & Row, 1969.

Pearce, Roy Harvey. "Yours Truly, Huck Finn." In *One Hundred Years of "Huckleberry Finn": The Boy, His Book, and American Culture,* ed. Robert Sattelmeyer and J. Donald Crowley. Columbia: University of Missouri Press, 1985.

Pease, Jane H., and William H. Pease. *They Who Would Be Free: Blacks' Search for Freedom, 1830–1861.* 1974. Reprint, Urbana: University of Illinois Press, 1990.

Perry, Thomas Sergeant. Review of *Adventures of Huckleberry Finn. Century Magazine* 30 (May 1885): 171–72. Reprinted in *Huck Finn among the Critics: A Centennial Selection,* ed. M. Thomas Inge. Frederick, Md.: University Publications of America, 1985.

Petit, Arthur G. *Mark Twain and the South.* Lexington: University Press of Kentucky, 1974.

Phillips, Ulrich B. *American Negro Slavery: A Survey of the Supply, Employment, and Control of Negro Labor as Determined by the Plantation Regime.* 1918. Reprint, Baton Rouge: Louisiana State University Press, 1966.

Phillips, Wendell. "Letter from Wendell Phillips, Esq." In *Narrative of the Life of Frederick Douglass, an American Slave. Written by Himself.* 1845. Reprint, New York: Anchor Books, 1973.

Pinckney, Darryl. *High Cotton.* 1992. Reprint, New York: Penguin, 1993.

Platt, Anthony M. *E. Franklin Frazier Reconsidered.* New Brunswick, N.J.: Rutgers University Press, 1991.

Puttock, Kay. "Historicism, *Huckleberry Finn,* and Howard Beach." *Teaching English in the Two-Year College* 17 (October 1990): 165–71.

Quirk, Tom. *Coming to Grips with "Huckleberry Finn": Essays on a Book, a Boy, and a Man.* Columbia: University of Missouri Press, 1993.

———. "Mark Twain." In *American Literary Scholarship: An Annual 1992,* ed. David J. Nordloh. Durham, N.C.: Duke University Press, 1994.

Raboteau, Albert J. *A Fire in the Bones: Reflections on African-American Religious History.* Boston: Beacon, 1995.

Railton, Stephen. "Jim and Mark Twain: What Do Dey Stan' For?" *Virginia Quarterly Review* 63 (Summer 1987): 393–408.

Rawick, George P. *From Sundown to Sunup: The Making of the Black Community.* Vol. 1 of *The American Slave: A Composite Autobiography.* Westport, Conn.: Greenwood, 1972.

Reichert, John. *Making Sense of Literature.* Chicago: University of Chicago Press, 1977.

Robinson, Forrest G. "The Characterization of Jim in *Huckleberry Finn.*" *Nineteenth-Century Literature* 43 (December 1988): 361–91.

Roediger, David R. *The Wages of Whiteness: Race and the Making of the American Working Class.* London: Verso, 1991.

Rubin, Louis D., Jr. *The Teller in the Tale.* Seattle: University of Washington Press, 1967.

Sack, Kevin. "In Little Rock, Clinton Warns of Racial Split." *New York Times,* September 26, 1997, A20.

Sanchez, Sonia. [Untitled]. *Interracial Books for Children Bulletin* 15, nos. 1–2 (1984): 11.

Sattelmeyer, Robert. "Interesting, but Tough." In *One Hundred Years of "Huckleberry Finn": The Boy, His Book, and American Culture,* ed. Robert Sattelmeyer and J. Donald Crowley. Columbia: University of Missouri Press, 1985.

Sattelmeyer, Robert, and J. Donald Crowley. *One Hundred Years of "Huckleberry Finn": The Boy, His Book, and American Culture.* Columbia: University of Missouri Press, 1985.

Saxton, Alexander. *The Rise and Fall of the White Republic: Class Politics and Mass Culture in Nineteenth-Century America.* London: Verso, 1990.

Schmitz, Neil. "The Paradox of Liberation in *Huckleberry Finn.*" *Texas Studies in Literature and Language* 13 (Spring 1971): 125–36.

Shapiro, Herbert. *White Violence and Black Response: From Reconstruction to Montgomery.* Amherst: University of Massachusetts Press, 1988.

Shulman, Robert. "Fathers, Brothers, and 'the Diseased': The Family, Individualism, and American Society in *Huck Finn.*" In *One Hundred Years of "Huckleberry Finn": The Boy, His Book, and American Culture,* ed. Robert Sattelmeyer and J. Donald Crowley. Columbia: University of Missouri Press, 1985.

Sigelman, Lee, and Susan Welch. *Black Americans' Views of Racial Inequality: The Dream Deferred.* Cambridge: Cambridge University Press, 1991.

Silber, Nina. *The Romance of Reunion: Northerners and the South, 1865–1900.* Chapel Hill: University of North Carolina Press, 1993.

Simon, Paul. *Freedom's Champion: Elijah Lovejoy.* Carbondale: Southern Illinois University Press, 1994.

Sloane, David E. E. *"Adventures of Huckleberry Finn": American Comic Vision.* Boston: Twayne Publishers, 1988.

Smiley, Jane. "Say It Ain't So, Huck: Second Thoughts on Mark Twain's 'Masterpiece.'" *Harper's,* January 1996, pp. 61–67.

Smith, David L. "Huck, Jim, and American Racial Discourse." *Black Writers on "Adventures of Huckleberry Finn" One Hundred Years Later,* ed. Thadious M. Davis. *Mark Twain Journal* 22 (Fall 1984): 4–12. Reprinted in *Satire or Evasion? Black Perspectives on "Huckleberry Finn,"* ed. James S. Leonard, Thomas A. Tenney, and Thadious M. Davis. Durham, N.C.: Duke University Press, 1992.

Smith, Henry Nash. Introduction to *Adventures of Huckleberry Finn,* ed. Smith. Boston: Houghton Mifflin, 1958.

———. "A Sound Heart and a Deformed Conscience." From *Mark Twain: The Development of a Writer.* 1962. Reprinted in *Adventures of Huckleberry Finn,* ed. Sculley Bradley et al. Norton Critical Edition. 2nd ed. New York: Norton, 1977.

Solomon, Andrew. "Jim and Huck: Magnificent Misfits." *Mark Twain Journal* 16 (Winter 1972): 17–24.

Spillers, Hortense J. "Changing the Letter: The Yokes, the Jokes of Discourse, or Mrs. Stowe, Mr. Reed." In *Slavery and the Literary Imagination,* ed. Deborah E. McDowell and Arnold Rampersad. Baltimore: Johns Hopkins University Press, 1989.

Stampp, Kenneth M. *The Peculiar Institution: Slavery in the Ante-Bellum South.* 1956. Reprint, New York: Vintage, 1989.

Stein, Ruth. "The ABC's of Counterfeit Classics: Adapted, Bowdlerized, and Condensed." *English Journal* 55 (December 1966): 1160–63.

Steinbrink, Jeffrey. "Who Wrote *Huckleberry Finn?* Mark Twain's Control of the Early Manuscript." In *One Hundred Years of "Huckleberry Finn": The Boy, His Book, and American Culture,* ed. Robert Sattelmeyer and J. Donald Crowley. Columbia: University of Missouri Press, 1985.

Stone, Albert E., Jr. *The Innocent Eye: Childhood in Mark Twain's Imagination.* New Haven: Yale University Press, 1961.

"Suggestions for Classroom Discussions of *Huck Finn.*" *Interracial Books for Children Bulletin* 15, nos. 1–2 (1984): 12.

Sundquist, Eric J. *To Wake the Nations: Race in the Making of American Literature.* Cambridge: Harvard University Press, 1993.

Takaki, Ronald T. *Violence in the Black Imagination: Essays and Documents.* Expanded ed. New York: Oxford University Press, 1993.

Thompson, Charles Miner. "Mark Twain as an Interpreter of American Character." *Atlantic Monthly,* April 1897, pp. 443–50.

Toll, Robert C. *Blacking Up: The Minstrel Show in Nineteenth-Century America.* New York: Oxford University Press, 1974.

Trilling, Lionel. From introduction to *Adventures of Huckleberry Finn.* 1948. Reprinted as "The Greatness of *Huckleberry Finn*" in *Adventures of Huckleberry Finn,* ed. Sculley Bradley et al. Norton Critical Edition. 2nd ed. New York: Norton, 1977.

Trollope, Frances. *Domestic Manners of the Americans.* 1832. Reprint, ed. Donald Smalley, New York: Vintage Books, 1960.

Twain, Mark. *Adventures of Huckleberry Finn.* Ed. Walter Blair and Victor Fischer. Berkeley: University of California Press, 1988.

———. *The Adventures of Tom Sawyer.* New York: Vintage/Library of America, 1991.

———. *The Autobiography of Mark Twain.* Ed. Charles Neider. New York: Harper & Row, 1959.

———. *Life on the Mississippi.* 1883. Reprint, ed. John Seelye, Oxford: Oxford University Press, 1990.

———. "Mark Twain's Working Notes." In *Adventures of Huckleberry Finn,* ed. Walter Blair and Victor Fischer. Berkeley: University of California Press, 1988.

———. "Only a Nigger." Editorial. *Buffalo Express,* August 26, 1869, p. 2. Reprinted in *Mark Twain: Social Critic,* by Philip S. Foner. New York: International Publishers, 1958.

———. "The Suppressed Passages." Ed. Willis Wager. In *Life on the Mississippi,* ed. Edward Wagenknecht. New York: Heritage Press, 1944.

———. "A True Story, Repeated Word for Word as I Heard It." 1874. Reprinted in *The Complete Short Stories of Mark Twain,* ed. Charles Neider. New York: Bantam, 1958.

———. "The United States of Lyncherdom." 1923. Reprinted in *Mark Twain and the Three R's: Race, Religion, Revolution—and Related Matters,* ed. Maxwell Geismar. Indianapolis: Bobbs-Merrill, 1973.

Wagenknecht, Edward. *Mark Twain: The Man and His Work.* Rev. ed. Norman: University of Oklahoma Press, 1961.

Walker, Nancy. "Reformers and Young Maidens: Women and Virtue in *Adventures of Huckleberry Finn.*" In *One Hundred Years of "Huckleberry Finn": The Boy, His Book, and American Culture,* ed. Robert Sattelmeyer and J. Donald Crowley. Columbia: University of Missouri Press, 1985.

Wallace, John H. "The Case against *Huck Finn.*" In *Satire or Evasion? Black Perspectives on "Huckleberry Finn,"* ed. James S. Leonard, Thomas A. Tenney, and Thadious M. Davis. Durham, N.C.: Duke University Press, 1992.

Watkins, Mel. *On the Real Side: Laughing, Lying, and Signifying—the Under-*

ground Tradition of African-American Humor That Transformed American Culture from Slavery to Richard Pryor. New York: Simon & Schuster, 1994.

Webber, Thomas L. *Deep Like the Rivers: Education in the Slave Quarter Community, 1831–1865.* New York: Norton, 1978.

Wells-Barnett, Ida B. "The Offense." In *Southern Horrors: Lynch Law in All Its Phases,* by Wells-Barnett. 1892. Reprinted in *Selected Works of Ida B. Wells-Barnett,* comp. Trudier Harris. New York: Oxford University Press, 1991.

Williamson, Joel. *The Crucible of Race: Black-White Relations in the American South since Emancipation.* New York: Oxford University Press, 1984.

Woodard, Fredrick, and Donnarae MacCann. "*Huckleberry Finn* and the Traditions of Blackface Minstrelsy." *Interracial Books for Children Bulletin* 15, nos. 1–2 (1984): 4–13.

Yarborough, Richard. "Strategies of Black Characterization in *Uncle Tom's Cabin* and the Early Afro-American Novel." In *New Essays on "Uncle Tom's Cabin,"* ed. Eric J. Sundquist. Cambridge: Cambridge University Press, 1986.

Yellin, Jean Fagan. Preface and Introduction to Harriet A. Jacobs, *Incidents in the Life of a Slave Girl: Written by Herself,* ed. Yellin. Cambridge: Harvard University Press, 1987.

Index

48; and Pap's diatribe, 72, 136n. 10; in *Tom Sawyer*, 26, 123n. 5; in witch-trick episode, 28
Missouri: abolitionism in, 141n. 9; free blacks in, 71; French control of, 52; identity of, 135n. 5; slave patrols in, 30
Mitchell, Lee Clark, 50
Morrison, Toni, 14, 21, 48, 90, 94, 109, 111
Moses, Paul, 111, 114
Mulattoes, 50–51, 71–72, 131n.15, 136nn. 8, 9
Myrdal, Gunnar, 68

NAACP, 3, 4, 10–11
Narrative of the Life of Frederick Douglass, 35, 132n. 2
Narrative of William Wells Brown, 37
Narrative voice, 15–16, 17–18, 91, 104–5, 145n. 8; and Huck's rebelliousness, 21–23; in Wilks episode, 78–79
Nat *(Huckleberry Finn)*, 96
Nativism, 69
Nell, W. C., 132n. 21
New York Board of Education, 4–5, 7, 120n. 5
"Nigger," 8–9, 12, 91, 92, 105–7; and black "mask," 146n. 13; excision of, 119n. 5; "good/bad" dichotomy, 66–67, 96; W. E. B. Du Bois on, 106
Night Riders in Black Folk History (Fry), 29
Night rider tales, 29–31

O'Connor, William Van, 47
Officeholders, black, 97–98, 143n. 21
Osofsky, Gilbert, 36
Owsley, William, 137n. 18

Pap *(Huckleberry Finn)*. See Finn, Pap
Pennington, James W. C., 59–60, 133n.8
Perry, Thomas Sergeant, 89
Phelps, Sally *(Huckleberry Finn)*, 91, 101
Phelps, Silas *(Huckleberry Finn)*, 93

Phelps episode, 89–94, 100–101; as allegory, 14, 94–99
Phillips, Ulrich B., 35
Pike stereotype, 135n. 5
Pinchback, P. B. S., 143n. 33
Pinckney, Darryl, 108–9
Plessy, Homer, 99, 143n. 33
Plessy v. Ferguson, 95, 99
Poor whites, 57, 62–63, 73, 135n. 5, 136n. 11; and lynching, 75. *See also* Finn, Pap; Loftus, Judith
Post-Reconstruction era, *Huckleberry Finn* as allegory for, 14, 71, 74–75, 77, 94–99
Puttock, Kay, 111, 114

Quirk, Tom, 20, 77, 106, 108, 112, 129n. 7

Race, and American cultural discussion, 2, 117
Race relations, fictional/nonfictional parallels in, 2, 103–5, 117–18
Rachel, Aunt ("A True Story"), 145n. 8
Racial epithets. *See* "Nigger"
Racial stereotypes: and contending views of Jim, 13, 28–29, 32, 51–52; deliberate conformity to, 13, 27, 146n.13; "good/bad nigger" dichotomy, 66–67, 96; "happy slave" myth, 35–36, 145n. 8; in illustrations of Jim, 129n. 8; "ruined servant," 28, 29, 124n. 13; and skin color, 71–72; slave narratives' challenges to, 35. *See also* Minstrelsy
Railton, Stephen, 111
Rawick, George P., 133n. 9, 140n. 5
Reconstruction, 71, 76, 97–99, 138n. 20
Reichert, John, 90
Robinson, Forrest G., 28–29, 32, 55, 94, 128n. 31
Robinson, W. H., 134n. 17
Roediger, David, 69
Rogues, the *(Huckleberry Finn)*, 62–64, 66, 93, 133n. 12; in Wilks episode, 79, 80–81

About the Authors

Elaine Mensh and Harry Mensh are independent writers and the co-authors of *The IQ Mythology: Class, Race, Gender, and Inequality*, which won an Anisfield-Wolf Book Award in 1992 for books dealing with issues of race and diversity. Harry Mensh is from Sutton, West Virginia, Elaine Mensh from Chicago. They live in New York City.